Michael Collins

'The Man Who Won the War'

12/9/96

D0873395

Michael Collins

'The Man Who Won the War'

T. Ryle Dwyer

MERCIER PRESS

MERCIER PRESS
PO Box 5, 5 French Church Street, Cork
        and
16 Hume Street, Dublin 2

© T. Ryle Dwyer, 1990

ISBN 0 85342 931 6

A CIP record is available for this book from the British Library.

10 9 8 7 6 5 4 3

TO BOB AND ANNE MARIA

Printed in Ireland by Colour Books Ltd.

Contents

1. 'The Man Who Won the War'

In formally proposing the adoption of the Anglo-Irish Treaty on 19 December 1921 Arthur Griffith referred to Michael Collins as 'the man who won the war,' much to the annoyance of the Defence Minister Cathal Brugha, who questioned whether Collins 'had ever fired a shot at any enemy of Ireland.'

Amid cries of 'Shame' and 'Get on with the Treaty,' Brugha complained that Collins had originated the story that there was a price on his head, and had personally sought the press publicity which built him into 'a romantic figure' and 'a mystical character' that he was not. Most of those present sat through the tirade in stunned silence, because there was no real stature to his wrath, just spite.

Even Brugha's strongest critics – those who disagreed with what they believed was his grossly distorted assessment – accepted that he was telling the truth as he saw it. Collins has since been the subject of numerous books but nobody has ever documented a single instance in which he fired a shot at the British.

Yet when Griffith rose to wind up the debate he had begun three weeks earlier, he was making no apologies for the remark to which Brugha had taken such exception. 'He referred to what I said about Michael Collins – that he was the man who won the war,' Griffith explained. 'I said it, and I say it again; he was the man that made the situation; he was the man, and nobody knows better than I do how, during a year and a half he worked from six in the morning until two next morning. He was the man whose matchless energy, whose indomitable will carried Ireland through the terrible crisis; and though I have not now and never had an ambition about either political affairs or history, if my name is to go down in history I want it associated with the name of Michael Collins. Michael Collins was the man who fought the Black and Tan terror for twelve months, until England was forced to offer terms.'

The assembly erupted with a roar of approval and thunderous applause. It was without doubt the most emotional response of the whole debate. Those who had listened to Brugha's invective in embarrassed silence, jumped at the opportunity of disassociating themselves from the earlier embittered remarks.

Who was this Michael Collins, the man who could engender such passion, and what was his real role in the War of Independence? How was it that two unquestionably sincere, selfless individuals like Griffith and Brugha, could differ so strongly about this man?

Michael Collins was born on 18 October 1890 near the tiny County Cork hamlet of Sam's Cross, where his father had a sixty acre farm. He was the youngest of eight children. His father was already seventy-five years old, having been born in 1815, the year of the Battle of Waterloo.

It was a closely-knit family. Michael had a very normal childhood, though being the youngest of such a large family he tended to be rather spoiled. In later life people would remember him as having taken a particular delight in listening to old people reminiscing. 'Great age held something for me that was awesome,' he told Hayden Talbot. 'I was much fonder of old people in the darkness than of young people in the daylight.'

He was only six years old when his father died and his attachment to old people, no doubt, had something to do with his late father's own age. He was after all old enough to have been the boy's great grandfather.

As he grew up Michael could not remember what his father looked like, but he never forgot an incident that happened when he was with him one day. They were out in the fields and his father was standing on a stone wall from which he dislodged a stone accidentally. Michael remembered looking at the stone as it came towards him, but he figured that it would not hurt him because his father was responsible for moving it.

'Would you believe it?' his father would say. 'There he was, barefooted, and the stone rolling down on him, and him never so much as looking at it! And when I got the thing off his foot and asked him why he had stood there and let it hit him, what do you think he replied? He told me: "'T'was I who sent it down!'"'

'It's a true Collins he is.'

Michael's oldest brother, John, took over the family farm, but the mother and younger children remained on.

Michael went to Lisavaird National School, where the headmaster, Denis Lyons, had a formative influence on the boy's developing sense of nationalism. Lyons, he wrote in 1916, had a 'pride of Irishness which has always meant most to me'. The teacher and local blacksmith, James Santry, who regaled Collins with stories of past Irish rebellions, infused in him 'a pride of the Irish as a race'.

When they talked of the events of the nineteenth century, the Great Famine, the Young Ireland Rebellion, and the trauma of the 1870s and 1880s, they were talking about times through which his father had lived. His paternal grandparents went back well into the eighteenth century. Indeed his father's oldest brother was born in 1789, so the family lived through the Rebellions of 1798 and all the great events since. It was understandable that young Michael Collins would show a considerable interest in the period.

Lyons was obviously impressed with his young pupil, whom he described as 'exceptionally intelligent in observation and at figures'. Collins was a good reader with a striking concern about political matters and a 'more than a normal interest in things appertaining to the welfare of his country'. His current political idol was the man who would later credit him with winning the war. 'In Arthur Griffith there is a mighty force afoot in Ireland,' Collins wrote in one of his school essays in 1902.

Although Collins betrayed 'a certain restless in temperament', his teacher still portrayed him as 'able and willing to adjust himself to all circumstances'. Having finished national school, he went on to secondary school in Clonakilty to prepare for the civil service entrance examination. During the school-week he lived with his eldest sister, Margaret O'Driscoll. Her husband owned a local newspaper, and Michael helped out with the reporting, usually on hurling or football matches. While there he learned to type.

His best friend in those early days was Jack Hurley, whose sister married Michael's eldest brother, John, and so cemented an in-law relationship with the Collins family. The two boys were inseparable friends and often stayed the night at each other's home.

In July 1906 Collins went to London to take up a job with the Post Office Savings Bank. It was a natural move for an ambitious boy of his age, because there were little prospects for him in West Cork. His second eldest sister, Johanna, or Hannie, as he called her, was already in the civil service in London, and they lived together at 5 Netherwood Place, West Kensington.

'I had Irish friends in London before I arrived, and in the intervening years I had made many more friends among Irish residents in London,' he recalled later. 'For the most part we lived lives apart. We chose to consider ourselves outposts of our nation.' One of these friends was Jack Hurley, and his presence undoubtedly eased the transition to life in London. Collins retained a rather romantic view of Ireland.

'I stand for an Irish civilisation based on the people and embodying and maintaining the things – their habits, ways of thought, customs – that make them different – the sort of life I was brought up in,' he wrote. He and his friends never integrated into British society, and never wanted to. 'We were proud of isolation,' he said, 'and we maintained it to the end.'

'Once,' he explained some years later, 'a crowd of us were going along the Shepherd's Bush Road when out of a lane came a chap with a donkey – just the sort of donkey and just the sort of cart they have at home. He came out quite suddenly and abruptly and we all cheered him. Nobody who has not been an exile will understand me, but I stand for that.'

During the nine and a half formative years which Collins spent in London he took a very active part in the Irish life of the city. In 1907 he helped raise money when Arthur Griffith's new party, Sinn Féin, ran a candidate in a parliamentry by-election. The candidate, who had resigned his own seat in order to re-contest it on a Sinn Féin ticket, was defeated. Party supporters tried to put the gloss of moral victory on what was really a devastating defeat from which the party would not recover for years. During those years Collins remained active in the party and delivered a number of papers. Two that were specially memorable concerned the political role of 'The Catholic Church in Ireland', and his assessment of 'The Irish Famine of 1847'.

Like many young Irishmen he went through an anti-clerical phase during his adolescent years, and his paper on the Catholic Church raised some eyebrows, when he called for the extermination of the clergy. His paper on the famine was equally volatile, as he accused Britain of deliberately provoking the Great Famine. While his version was grossly distorted, his view was one that was widely shared by many of his fellow countrymen.

Collins became particularly active in the Gaelic Athletic Association (GAA). He enjoyed playing hurling with the Gerald-ines Club, usually playing at either wing back or centre field. Opponents remembered him as an effective, though not particularly polished player. He had a short temper, which often got the better of him, and he was a very poor loser.

Whether on the hurling field or elsewhere, Collins liked to have things his own way, which did not endear him to many of his contemporaries. As a result he faced keen competition when, at the age of seventeen, he made a successful bid for the post of secretary of the Geraldines Club.

The minutes of the club, which have been preserved in the National Library, make interesting reading. They show him to have been a committed and enthusiastic member, with an intense nationalistic outlook. He insisted on the club purchasing all jerseys and medals from Dublin firms. As one of the club's delegates to the London convention, he proposed that the practice of paying expenses for delegates should be dropped – thereby demonstrating both his commitment and his unselfishness. But, of course, he expected the same kind of dedication from others, and he was an absolute stickler when it came to club finances.

In his first formal report, he complained that the treasurer had pocketed the club finances for a time. 'The man's protracted retention of the club's money, and his brazen falsehoods in connection therewith' nearly cost the club its playing pitch, Collins explained. 'Eventually,' he continued, 'we got him to disgorge.' There was no elaboration on how the man was persuaded to pay up, but the word 'disgorge' seemed to have a rather painful ring to it. Not satisfied with simply getting the money back, Collins persuaded the meeting to expel the individual 'as an undesirable and untrustworthy member'.

Collins' initial secretary's report betrayed all the brashness and candid realism that were so much a part of his character. 'Our internal troubles were saddening,' he explained, 'but our efforts in football and hurling were perfectly heartbreaking. In no single contest have our colours been crowned with success. In hurling we haven't even the consolation of a creditable performance... I can only say that our record of the past half-year leaves no scope for self congratulation,' he concluded. 'Signs of decay are unmistakable, and if members are not prepared in the future to act more harmoniously together and more self-sacrificingly generally – the club will soon have faded into an inglorious and well-deserved oblivion.'

It was while club secretary that Collins got into his first political fight. It was over the question of banning members of the GAA from taking part in 'foreign games' like rugby or soccer. Most Irish people in England were anxious to play soccer, but Collins wanted the ban and vociferously opposed the idea of Irishmen playing soccer. He also resented Irish athletes competing for the United Kingdom in international events. In 1913, for example, he took exception when the controlling body of the GAA in London reinstated four Irishmen who had competed on the British team at the Olympic Games in 1912. Sport, as far as he was concerned, was not only a recreation, but also a political weapon.

Ever since Ireland became a part of the United Kingdom in 1801 Irish people had tended to look to London for things political, economic and recreational, but Collins believed the GAA, founded in 1885, had begun to reverse this trend by reminding Irish boys that they had a separate nationality. 'It provided and restored national games as an alternative to the slavish adoption of English sport,' he contended.

The most significant development of all, however, was the foundation of the Gaelic League in 1893. 'It checked the peaceful penetration and once and for all turned the minds of the Irish people back to their own country,' he wrote. 'It did more than any other movement to restore the national pride, honour, and self-respect.'

Collins' parents were both native Gaelic speakers, but they came to equate the Irish language with the economic backwardness of Gaeltacht areas, so they spoke English to their children. Michael started to learn Gaelic on a number of occasions but other events inevitably dominated his time.

His work, political and sporting activities all combined to take up a lot of time. Particularly prominent among his friends were Corkmen like Jack Hurley, or Joe O'Reilly, whom he met in London for the first time. Hurley was still his closest friend. 'We think the same way in Irish matters,' Collins wrote. 'At worst he is a boon companion. At best there is no one else I would have as a friend.'

Unlike most of his young contemporaries, Collins showed little interest in the opposite sex at this stage of his life. Except for his sister, he stayed in the company of men almost exclusively. 'The society of girls had apparently no attraction for him,' according to Piaras Beaslaí. 'He preferred the company of young men, and never paid any attention to the girls belonging to the Branch, not even to the sisters and friends of his male companions.'

Beaslaí, the only biographer who could claim to have been more than a passing acquaintance of Collins, noted that 'the usual philanderings and flirtations of young men of his age had little interest or attraction for him, though he sometimes amused himself by chaffing his young friends over their weaknesses in that direction.'

In later years some people – who never knew Collins – would suggest that he may have been homosexual. It has all been pure speculation, based largely on the portraits by Beaslaí and Frank O'Connor, though neither author ever actually suggested it.

O'Connor relied heavily on Collins' longtime friend Joe O'Reilly for his portrait, which showed Collins as a contradictory conglomeration of various characteristics – he was a buoyant, warm-hearted, fun-loving individual with a thoughtful, generous nature, but he was also a thoughtless, selfish, ill-mannered bully. While other young men went looking for a piece of ass, he was more inclined to go looking for 'a piece of ear'. He would burst into a room and jump on a colleague and wrestle him to the floor, and then begin biting the unfortunate friend's ear until the other fellow surrendered, often with blood streaming from his ear. It was certainly the portrait of a rather strange fellow.

During the War of Independence Collins frequently stayed at Vaughan's Hotel in Rutland (now Parnell) Square, where a room was reserved for men 'on the run'. 'He usually shared a bedroom with [Harry] Boland and myself,' Beaslaí wrote, 'and frequently shared Boland's bed with him.' Given the times and the circumstances there was nothing unusual about sharing a bed with a colleague. They were lucky to have a bed to share. When Collins stayed elsewhere, Beaslaí did not know about his sleeping arrangements. For much of the period, especially from 1919 to mid-1921 Collins had no fixed abode. He was a wanted man, and he purposely kept colleagues in the dark about where he stayed. If they could find him, then so could the police.

Afterwards it became possible to piece together some of his safe houses. Most were run by single women, the aunts or widowed mothers of colleagues. Others would later try to suggest that there was a sexual aspect to his relationship with those women, but no shred of evidence was produced to support this characterisation of him as a rampant philanderer. Those making the charge might just as easily have suggested that he or any other man who shared an apartment with a sister, were engaged in an incestuous relationship.

While in London, it was not unusual that Collins or any other person in similar circumstances – a working young man deeply involved in sport and politics – should show little interest in women for the time being. He was in no hurry to form an amorous attachment. After all his father was sixty years old before he married, and Michael would not be that age until 1950. In the trying times between the Easter Rebellion of 1916 and the Truce in 1921, he obviously could not have provided the home life for a wife that he had enjoyed within his own closely-knit family at Sam's Cross. Yet once things returned to near normality following the Truce, he quickly fell in love with Kitty Kiernan, and there were intimations in their correspondence that their relationship was consummated sexually, which would seem to demolish the homosexual accusation, as would rumours that he had an affair with Hazel Lavery, the wife of painter, Sir John Lavery, in London during the Treaty negotiations.

The evidence of this affair is totally from her side. She met Collins on a number of occasions and obviously wanted to have an affair with him. As she was an attractive woman – whose portrait later graced the first Irish pound note and still graces the water-mark on the Irish currency – he may well have availed of her sexual favours, but that is getting ahead of the story. During his emigrant days in London he clearly showed little interest in women, and was obviously more at home in the company of Corkmen. Through his involvement in the GAA he met Sam Maguire, a Corkman working for the Post Office. He persuaded Collins to join the Irish Republican Brotherhood (IRB) in 1909. It was a secret oath-bound society founded in the mid-nineteenth century and dedicated towards national freedom in the form of an independent Irish republic. This marked a moving away from the non-violence advocated by Sinn Féin to the forceful approach to the solution of the Irish question.

Collins argued that lack of organisation 'was chiefly responsible for the failure of several risings' and it was as an organiser that he would make his name in the coming years. 'A force organised on practical lines and headed by realists,' Collins wrote, 'would be of great consequence. Whereas a force organised on theoretical lines and headed by idealists, would, I think be a very doubtful factor'. His own organisational ability was recognised with his appointment as Treasurer of the south of England district of the IRB.

In 1910 Collins quit the Post Office Savings Bank to work for a stock brokerage firm, but after the outbreak of the Great War in 1914 he moved back into the civil service to work as a Labour Exchange clerk in Whitehall. He did not want to fight in the British army, but neither did he want 'the murky honour of being a conscientious objector,' and so he considered migrating to the United States. His brother, Patrick, was already there, and he encouraged Michael to cross the Atlantic. He went so far as to obtain a job with an American firm, the Guarantee Trust Company of New York, in April 1915.

With his personal conscription crisis coming to a head in early 1916, he decided to return to Ireland, where the IRB was planning to stage a rebellion, using the Irish Volunteer Force (IVF) in which Collins had been enrolled by his friend Jack Hurley in 1914. On handing in his notice he told his employers he was going 'to join up.' They naturally assumed he was joining the British army when he left London for Ireland on 15 January.

He lost little time in Dublin contacting two of the IRB leaders, Tom Clarke and Seán MacDermott, who were the driving inspiration behind the planned rebellion. At the outbreak of the Great War in 1914, the Supreme Council of the IRB decided to exploit Britain's difficulties by staging a rebellion, and Clarke and MacDermott were selected to look into the situation. They were authorised to co-opt anyone they wished on to their little committee, which eventually became known as the Military Council.

The first person they enlisted was Patrick Pearse, a shy, self-contained individual who was probably the most effective public speaker in the country. A poet, playwright, lawyer and educator, they turned the leadership of the Military Council over to him. Others later added to the council included Joseph Mary Plunkett and James Connolly, the militant labour organiser who was included to forestall his Irish Citizen Army from embarking on a separate rebellion.

Collins was assigned as an aide to Joseph Mary Plunkett, the chief military strategist of the rebellion. A slender, pale, sickly young man with absolutely no military experience; all of what he knew about military strategy had been gleaned from books or from his own fertile imagination. He was a poet with a romantic vision and a desperate need to leave his mark on a world in which he was not destined to stay long. He was already dying of tuberculosis.

While looking for a job in Dublin, Collins got a temporary part-time position as a financial adviser to Plunkett's sister, Geraldine, who still lived with her parents in Kimmage. Some fifty of the London-Irish Volunteers were staying on their grounds, making up what Pearse would call a standing army.

The aim of the Military Council was to proclaim an Irish Republic and set up a Provisional Government on Easter Sunday, 23 April 1916. Using the combined forces of the Irish Volunteers, Citizen Army, and Hibernian Rifles, they would seize prominent buildings throughout Dublin and hold them for as long as possible A consignment of German arms was to be landed the same day near Tralee, for Volunteers in the rest of the country to rise in conjunction with the rebellion in Dublin.

Much of the negotiations with Germany had been conducted through John Devoy of Clan na Gael, the IRB's sister organisation in the United States, but the British Admiralty had broken the German codes and were reading the messages between New York and Berlin, with the result that British naval intelligence knew well in advance of the rebellion planned for Easter Sunday, and of the plan to land arms. The British also knew that Roger Casement – who had gone to Berlin as an emissary of the IRB – was returning to Ireland by submarine. The Royal Navy duly intercepted the ship carrying the arms and Casement was arrested soon after coming ashore near Tralee.

He had not returned to take part in a rebellion, as was generally supposed; rather, he wanted to stop it. He asked to be allowed to appeal to his colleagues to call the whole thing off because he realised it was doomed to failure, but Admiral William 'Blinker' Hall, the chief of naval intelligence, wanted the rebellion to go ahead. He had already been withholding information about the planned uprising from the Dublin Castle authorities in order that the rebellion would take place and the British government could then be manipulated into introducing the repressive measures that he thought desirable in Ireland. 'It is better that a cankering sore like this should be cut out,' Hall told Casement in London on Easter Sunday when the latter pleaded to be allowed to use his influence to call off the rebellion.

Although the rebels would be drawn mainly from the IVF, Eoin MacNeill, the leader, had been kept in the dark by the IRB people, who secretly controlled his organisation. It was they who had initially decided to set up the IVF in the first place and had merely turned to him because – as a professor of early Irish history and president of the Gaelic League – he provided a cover of academic respectability. They thought they could always manipulate him in furthering their aims. Whereas he looked on the Irish Volunteers essentially as a means of counteracting the influence of the Ulster Volunteer Force in order to keep the pressure on Westminster to grant home rule to Ireland, the IRB leaders were looking for much more than a devolved parliament within the United Kingdom framework. They wanted a sovereign, independent, Irish republic, and they saw the Irish Volunteers as a potential army to drive the British out of Ireland.

For months the Irish Volunteers had been drilling and marching publicly, with the result that little notice was taken when the organisation called for nationwide parades on Easter Sunday. Only when the men would get together on that day would they be told of the rebellion.

MacNeill learned of the plans on the Wednesday beforehand, and he threatened to call the whole thing off but Pearse managed to persuade him to go along with the Military Council on assuring him that arrangements had been made to secure German help. By Saturday, however, it became apparent that this help would not be coming following Casement's arrest and the interception of the arms' ship by the Royal Navy. MacNeill therefore decided to call off the rebellion. He sent out messengers with orders to suspend all manoeuvres planned for Sunday, and he put a notice to the same effect in the *Sunday Independent*.

The rebellion had been called off and Sunday passed without incident, but the IRB leaders were now desperate. With the capture of Casement, it was obviously only a matter of time before they would be rounded up. They therefore quietly sent word to the Dublin battalions that the postponed manoeuvres would take place at noon the following day, Monday, 24 April. The British were caught totally by surprise, which was understandable because so were MacNeill and the vast majority of those the IRB hoped would take part.

2. 'We Lost, Didn't We?'

Collins spent Easter Sunday night in a Dublin hotel with Joseph Mary Plunkett, who was so weak that he needed help dressing in the morning. Afterwards Collins went out to Kimmage to join the London contingent.

Dressed in his staff captain's uniform, he looked smart, especially in comparison to the others, clad in ill-fitting military outfits, which were an assortment of different shades of green and were anything but uniform. He was not impressed with them and flushed with anger when they – irritated by his smug air of self-importance – retaliated by sniggering at his appearance.

Around eleven o'clock the fifty-seven men boarded a tram for the city centre at Harold's Cross; they were a rather motley bunch, some with bandoleers, and laden with rifles, and pistols, as well as pick-axes, sledge-hammers and shovels. A woman passenger was upset at being prodded by the rifle of one heavily laden man who insisted in sitting down beside her without removing any of his equipment.

'Fifty-seven two-penny fares, and don't stop until we reach O'Connell Bridge,' the officer in charge told the conductor as he handed over the exact money.

One of the Volunteers sat down with his rifle nonchalantly pointed at the head of the driver, who ignored the pleas of passengers wishing to alight as he raced by their stops on the way to the city centre.

There was an air of farce about the proceedings as the men formed up outside Liberty Hall. Pearse was about to take his place at the head of the group when he was embarrassed by one of his sisters.

'Come home, Patrick, and leave all this foolishness!' she pleaded.

Pearse blushed with embarrassment, and the men around him shuffled nervously.

'Form Four,' Connolly shouted and ordered the men to march off, giving Pearse the excuse to brush past his sister to the head of the group marching off towards Sackville Street.

Plunkett, Connolly and Pearse formed the first line, with

more than three hundred men marching four abreast behind them. Brennan Whitmore was on the extreme left with Collins on his immediate inside. Clarke and MacDermott did not consider themselves soldiers so they followed on the pavement.

It was a holiday and the streets were relatively quiet. Onlookers, now used to such parades, did not realise anything unusual was happening until the men reached the General Post Office (GPO), and Connolly gave the order to charge the building. The staff and customers were ordered out unceremoniously. Some left reluctantly, muttering in resentment as they were hustled out the door. Lieutenant Chambers of the Royal Fusiliers was sending a telegram to his wife when the men charged in, and Plunkett ordered that he be taken prisoner. Collins went to the telephone booth and yanked out the flex, which he used to tie up the unfortunate officer whom he lifted bodily and dumped in the telephone booth with a laugh.

'Please don't shoot me,' pleaded Constable Dunphy of the Dublin Metropolitan Police (DMP) as he was taken prisoner. 'I done no harm.'

'We don't shoot prisoners,' replied Collins, who ordered two Volunteers to bring the man upstairs and lock him in a room.

When Connolly ordered the ground floor windows to be knocked out, Collins took a boyish delight in smashing the glass.

'Glory be to God!' cried a startled women outside. Huddled in a black shawl, she looked on in amazement. 'Would you look at them smashing all the lovely windows!' Collins laughed boisterously and the men around him joined in his laughter.

Pearse went outside and, as a small group looked on indifferently, proclaimed the Irish Republic 'in the name of God and of the dead generations'. Inside the men continued with their task of fortifying the building for the expected counter-attack. Collins and Whitmore were detailed to ensure all windows were properly barricaded.

Rumours abounded in the GPO both on that day and for the rest of the week. There were unfounded reports that the Germans had landed, that a fleet of German submarines were blockading Dublin Bay to ensure the British could not bring in reinforcements, that the Turks had landed in Waterford and that Big Jim Larkin was returning from the United States with a force of 50,000 Irish-Americans. One of Connolly's men rushed into the GPO to announce that King George and Lord Kitchener had been captured. 'In the Henry Street Waxworks!' he added after a calculated pause.

The only real engagement that those in the GPO had with the enemy on the first day was when a company of British Lancers rode down Sackville Street in formation on horseback, apparently hoping that their intimidatory appearance would frighten the rebels. It was an absurd gesture. When the firing began three of the horsemen and two of their horses were shot dead and another man fell mortally wounded, while the remainder bolted for safety.

'If that's the way they attack a fortified building,' one of the rebels cried, 'there's some hope for us yet.'

The Lancers had not even fired a shot, but the insurgents suffered a number of casualties anyway. A volunteer in a building across the street was killed in the cross-fire, and another was injured on the GPO side, while a third shot himself in the stomach accidentally. The British officer dumped by Collins in the telephone booth, had a narrow escape when a stray bullet lodged in the timber inches from his head. His bonds were duly cut, and he was sent to join other prisoners upstairs.

The second day was largely one of anticipation as the rebels waited for the British to attack, while an orgy of looting was taking place outside throughout Sackville Street. Realising that the police would not dare enter the street, people from the nearby slums broke display windows and helped themselves to whatever they desired in the shops. Pearse went out to the foot of Nelson's Pillar in front of the GPO and denounced the looters as 'hangers-on of the British army'.

'The country is rising in answer to Dublin's call, and the final achievement of Ireland's freedom is now, with God's help, only a matter of days,' he declared in this address to the citizens of Dublin. 'The valour, self-sacrifice, and discipline of Irish men and women are about to win our country a glorious place among the nations.'

Wednesday dawned with still no sign of the expected British assault, but as the morning progressed there were sounds of shelling when the gunship *Helga* opened up on Liberty Hall. The men had not expected the shelling. Connolly, a dedicated Marxist, had confidently predicted the forces of British capitalism would be so anxious to avoid damaging property that they would not use artillery on expensive buildings but storm them with troops instead.

The men in the Eden Quay area were ordered to abandon their positions and move to the GPO, only to find that the messenger who had brought the order had been confused, Connolly had not wanted them to retreat at all. They therefore had to make their perilous way back across Sackville Street amid heavy British sniperfire. The incident was indicative of the confusion that reigned in Republican ranks throughout the week.

There were unfounded rumours the British were preparing to attack the GPO with gas, so one of the men with some chemical training was assigned to prepare an antidote. He put together a concoction and distributed it throughout the building in buckets.

'What the hell good will that do?' Collins asked him.

'None,' the man conceded, and that put an end to the idiotic scheme.

Collins was much too practical to waste time on such matters. He was actually singled out as 'the most active and efficient officer in the place', by Desmond FitzGerald, who had been placed in charge of the GPO canteen.

Having been ordered to economise rigidly to ensure that the food supply would last for three weeks, FitzGerald irritated many of the men by providing only meagre portions, but Collins was not about to put up with petty restrictions. He came in one morning with some men who had been working hard on demolishing walls and building barricades. He told FitzGerald the men were to be fed properly even if it meant that they took all the remaining food.

'I did not attempt to argue with him,' FitzGerald related. 'The men sat down openly rejoicing that I had been crushed. Apparently some of them had already been the victims of my rigid economy.'

The most difficult time for soldiers is invariably while waiting for a battle to begin, and those in the GPO had to wait for the best part of four days. Every so often someone brought news of British troops massing for an attack but each time the report turned out to be a false alarm, and this inevitably began to affect morale. At one point on the Wednesday night Connolly tried to raise the men's spirits with a song. He began:

> We'll sing a song, a soldier's song
>   With cheering, rousing chorus,
> As round the blazing fires we throng,

The starry heavens o'er us.
Impatient for the coming fight,
    And as we wait the morning's light,
Here in the silence of the night
    We'll chant a soldier's song.

Others joined in the ensuing chorus as it built to a crescendo with some fifty voices belting out what would one day become the country's National Anthem:

Soldiers are we, whose lives are pledged to Ireland;
    Some have come from a land beyond the wave;
Sworn to be free, no more our ancient sireland
    Shall shelter the despot, or the slave.
Tonight we man the *bearna baoghail*
    In Erin's cause, come woe or weal;
'Mid cannon's roar and rifle's peal
    We'll chant a soldier's song.

Collins, who had been sleeping when the singing began, awoke looking decidedly perturbed. 'If this is supposed to be a concert,' he said factitiously to Connolly's secretary Winifred Carney, 'they'll want the piano in the back room.'

The weather next day was glorious with a slight breeze from the east, blowing over the putrefying carcasses of the two dead horses outside on the street. Having knocked out all the glass in the windows of the GPO the men had to endure the nauseating stench while the interminable waiting for an assault continued. The British never did attack as Plunkett and Connolly had anticipated, instead they began shelling Sackville Street with heavy artillery placed a short distance away in Rutland Square. Before long the east side of the street was in flames.

Connolly led some men out of the GPO on a raid but was wounded in the process. Pearse, meanwhile, was busy preparing an address that he delivered to all the available men in the main hall of the GPO that evening. Although it was supposedly a pep talk for the troops, it was really an address to posterity over the heads of the gathered men to whom he referred in the third person throughout.

'Let me, who have led them into this, speak in my own name, and in my fellow commandants' names, and in the name of Ireland present and to come, their praise, and ask those who come after them to remember them,' he said. 'They have held out for four days against the might of the British Empire. They have established Ireland's right to be called a Republic, and they have established this government's right to sit at the peace table at the end of the European war.'

Collins basically had little time for Pearse, an impractical dreamer, politically inexperienced, militarily innocent and obsessed with mystical visions of a blood sacrifice. Writing in December 1915, Pearse had described the first sixteen months of the Great War as 'the most glorious' period of European history.

'Heroism has come back to the earth,' he wrote. 'The old heart of the earth needed to be warmed with the red wine of the battlefields. Such august homage was never before offered to God as this, the homage of millions of lives gladly given for love of country.' He wrote this blasphemous twaddle as if he were experiencing some kind of spiritual orgasm.

A medium-sized man with a handsome face, marred by a pronounced cast in his right eye which usually prompted him to ensure his photograph was taken in profile to conceal his cockeyed appearance, Pearse had a messianic complex. It was more than mere coincidence that he selected Easter Sunday for the rising. Just as Christ had sacrificed himself to save mankind, Pearse believed he was sacrificing himself as a means of saving the Irish people's sacred right to nationhood. Just why the son of an Englishman should take such a task upon himself, one can only ponder.

Although a general in the rebel army, he had more of the mentality of a scout master, with some rather strange ideas. He advocated that parents should dress their sons in kilts, which might not have seemed so strange, if he had not shown transvestite tendencies himself as a youngster by dressing in his sister's clothes, and some of his later writings betrayed distinct homosexual inclinations – such as the following excerpt from his poem, *Little Lad of the Tricks*:

> I forgive you, child
> Of the soft red mouth:
> I will not condemn anyone
> For a sin not understood.
>
> Raise your comely head
> Till I kiss your mouth:

If either of us is the better of that
I am the better of it.

There is a fragrance in your kiss
That I have not found yet
In the kisses of women
Or in the honey of their bodies.

Other writings betrayed an extreme attitude when it came to
proving manhood. 'Bloodshed is a cleansing and a sanctifying
thing,' he wrote, 'and the nation which regards it as the final
horror has lost its manhood.' In his case, it was as if he was going
to prove his masculinity by shedding his own blood.

Looking back on Easter week some months later, Collins
would be quite critical of Pearse. 'I do not think the Rising week
was an appropriate time for the issue of memoranda couched in
poetic phrase, nor of actions worked out in similar fashion,' he
wrote. 'It had the air of a Greek tragedy about it, the illusion
being more or less completed with the issue of the before
mentioned memoranda. Of Pearse and Connolly I admire the
latter the most.'

While Connolly shared Pearse's enthusiasm for the rebellion,
he had a saner view of the horror of war. 'We do not think that
the old heart of the earth needs to be warmed with the red wine
of millions of lives,' he wrote in response to Pearse's obnoxious
drivel about the Great War. 'We think anyone who does is a
blithering idiot'.

'Connolly was a realist, Pearse the direct opposite,' according
to Collins. 'There was an air of earthy directness about Connolly. It impressed me. I would have followed him through hell
had such action been necessary. But I honestly doubt very much
if I would have followed Pearse – not without some thought
anyway.'

Collins also thought highly of two of the other leaders, Clarke
and MacDermott. Not being soldiers, they went into and remained in the GPO as excited spectators rather than partici-
pants. 'Both were built on the best foundations,' according to
Collins, who was especially impressed by MacDermott. 'Wherever he walked there went with him all the shades of the great
Irishmen of the past. He was God-given. He was humble in the
knowledge of his own greatness and in the task which he had
chosen to do. He did not seek glory as a personal investment but

as a National investment.'

In writing to friends about the rebellion, it was particularly noticeable that Collins never mentioned the fifth and only other man of the Military Council in the GPO, Joseph Mary Plunkett. Maybe his reticence had something to do with a sense of loyalty to the man for whom he had been an aide. Plunkett, like Pearse, was a poet over-given to a sense of the dramatic, and his jewellery – a bangle on a wrist and a large antique ring on one of his fingers – seemed incongruous with military masculinity. In addition, he was physically weak and tired very easily. It was only three weeks since he had an operation for the glandular tuberculosis that was obviously killing him, with the result that he spent a great deal of time resting in the GPO.

'On the whole I think the Rising was bungled terribly costing many a good life,' Collins explained. 'It seemed at first to be well organised, but afterwards became subjected to panic decisions and a great lack of very essential organisation and co-operation.'

On Friday, the fifth day of the rebellion, the British began firing incendiary shells at the GPO. Collins and a large detail of men held the fire at bay for as long as possible, putting barriers of sand across doorways and flooding the floors with water, but this was only a delaying measure. The fire gradually took hold and it became necessary to evacuate the building. Pearse called all the available men together to deliver another of his addresses in the main hall.

'If we have accomplished no more than we have accomplished, I am satisfied,' he told them. 'We should have accomplished the task of enthroning as well as proclaiming the Irish Republic as a sovereign state, had our arrangements for a simultaneous Rising of the whole country – with a combined plan as sound as the Dublin plan has proved to be – been allowed to go through on Easter Sunday. Of the fatal countermanding order which prevented those plans being carried out, I shall not speak further. Both Eoin MacNeill and we have acted in the best interests of Ireland.'

With the fire in the GPO out of control, it was decided to move the headquarters to a factory on Great Britain Street, but Pearse took the decision without making any enquiries about the positioning of enemy forces in the area. The O'Rahilly and some men went to make preparations and had only just left when one of the Volunteers told Pearse that Great Britain Street had been solidly in the hands of the Crown forces since Thursday.

'Stop The O'Rahilly,' Pearse shouted. 'He's gone into Moore Street with some men.'

Collins darted out the door and ran up Henry Place, but he was too late. The O'Rahilly had already been cut down. Collins and those who followed him took refuge in the terraced cottages lining Moore Street, where they were joined by the other survivors of the headquarters' staff. Pearse had led them from the burning building with his sword drawn and held aloft in a heroic gesture, symbolic of his own impracticality.

For a time the Volunteers tried to reach the British barricade at the top of the street by breaking a passageway in the walls of the terraced houses, but the idea of setting up a new headquarters in the factory in Great Britain Street was clearly no longer feasible. Pearse therefore looked for surrender terms next morning.

The British insisted on 'an unconditional surrender', and Pearse decided to concede, though some of the Kimmage contingent wanted to fight on. Clarke tried to convince them but failed, as did Plunkett.

'If you fight on,' Collins pleaded, 'you'll do nothing but seal the death warrants for all our leaders.'

'Sure, they'll all be shot anyway,' someone replied. In desperation, Collins asked MacDermott to talk to them.

'Now what is it you fellows intend to do?' MacDermott asked them. He listened patiently to their arguments and then tried to persuade them to surrender, mentioning some civilians shot that morning.

'We're hopelessly beaten,' MacDermott said. 'We haven't a prayer of fighting our way out of here. You've already fought a gallant fight, every one of you. You gain nothing, you lose everything if you try to continue. You think you'll be killed, do you, if you surrender. Not at all.

'Some of the rest of us will be killed, but none of you,' he continued. 'Why should they kill you? And why should they put you in the British army? You'd be no good to them. They'll send you to prison for a few years, that's the worst. But what does it matter, if you survive? The thing you must do, all of you, is survive, come back, carry on the work so nobly begun this week. Those of us who are shot can die happy if we know you'll be living on to finish what we started.'

Nobody else had anything to say. The men who had returned from Britain to take part in the Rising relented. 'I know you wanted to fight on, and I'm proud of you,' MacDermott said. 'I know also that this week of Easter will never be forgotten. Ireland will one day be free because of what you've done here.'

They then ate what was left of their rations and said the rosary, some holding a rifle in one hand, and a rosary beads in the other.

Collins marched out with the headquarters staff into Sackville Street and turned left up towards the Parnell monument where they downed arms and surrendered. They were joined by men from the Four Courts and then marched up to the green in front of the Rotunda Hospital, where they were herded together and surrounded by a ring of soldiers with bayonets at the ready.

The officer in charge of the Crown forces was Captain Lea Wilson, a florid-faced, thick-lipped Englishman, who behaved as if he had a little too much to drink. He roared at his own men and issued contradictory orders while rushing from one prisoner to another, shouting that he was going to have them shot. He singled Clarke out for particularly harsh treatment.

'That old bastard is the Commander-in-Chief. He keeps a tobacco shop across the street. Nice general for your fucking army.' He had Clarke stripped naked and prodded the man mercilessly, while nurses looked on from the windows of the Rotunda. Collins watched on in indignation.

'A dark night, a dark lane, a stout stick – and that fellow!' one Volunteer was heard to mutter. Collins never forgave Wilson for what he did to Clarke. Four years later he would take particular delight in having Wilson killed in revenge for what he had done that day.

On Sunday morning the prisoners were marched to Richmond Barracks, through streets lined with irate citizens who pelted them with rotten fruit and vegetables. Holding the rebels totally responsible, the Irish people were incensed at the damage caused by the Rebellion in which more innocent civilians perished than anybody else. Two hundred and sixty-two civilians were reported killed, while the Crown forces suffered 141 dead, and 62 rebels were killed in the fighting. Among the latter was Collins' great friend, Jack Hurley.

'Do you think they'll let us go,' a Volunteer asked as they were being walked though the hostile crowd of onlookers.

'Bejasus, I hope not,' replied a colleague.

'The citizens of Dublin would have torn us to pieces,' wrote Desmond Ryan.

The prisoners were taken to the gymnasium at Richmond Barracks, where police detectives circulated among them, picking out known activists for special treatment. They were Irishmen singling out other Irishmen for trial and in some cases, execution.

Collins had only been in Dublin for three months, so he was not known to the detectives. At one point he thought he heard his name being called in one corner of the gym, and he walked there to find himself among a group about to be shipped directly to Britain. That evening he and 488 other prisoners were marched to the North Wall.

'Well it was a good fight, Mick,' a colleague said as they were going down the Quays.

'What, do you mean a good fight?' he snapped in reply. 'We lost, didn't we?'

The men were herded together on a cattle boat and deported, with the result that he was out of the country and would not learn for some time of the way in which the British over-reacted in the following days.

In addition to rounding up the rebels, they arrested and deported hundreds of people who had taken no part in the rebellion, people like Eoin MacNeill and Arthur Griffith, the founder of Sinn Féin. Only about 1,600 people had taken part on the rebel side, but the Crown authorities arrested over 3,200 people and proceeded to deport more than 2,500 of them.

The wholesale arrests and the sixteen executions that followed were a terrible blunder on Britain's part because they generated enormous compassion which turned to sympathy for the rebels. In death Pearse – notwithstanding his demented view of the world – became a national hero and his mystical rhetoric coloured the perception of what he had tried to do. Henceforth the rebellion would be seen in the terms of a kind of religious experience. The executed were referred to as 'martyrs' and it was said that the executions 'helped to convert' the Irish people to the separatist cause. The rebellion itself would become known as the Easter Rising, and in the process Pearse's accomplishment would be symbolically equated with the greatest of all Christ's miracles.

3. 'In the End They'll Despair'

Upon arrival in Holyhead, the prisoners found two trains waiting for them on either side of the railway platform. One went to Knutsford and the other, which Collins boarded, to Stafford.

He and 288 other rebels were marched from the railroad station to Stafford Military Detention Barracks. At one point on the way a couple of by-standers tried to attack one of the prisoners, but was driven off by a burly English sergeant.

'Get back you, bastards,' he shouted at the assailants. 'These men fought for their country, you won't.'

For three weeks the prisoners were kept in solitary confinement, and only allowed out for short periods to walk in single file around a court yard in total silence. They had no news of the outside world.

In the monotony of this daily routine, each man got to know his cell intimately, the stone floor, thirty-five panes of glass and the black iron door. They had a slate to write on, a pencil, a bedboard, a stool, a table, a can, a bowl, a glass, and endless time to think. They could hear the noise of the town in the distance.

'It was for the most part an unpremeditated solitary confinement,' Desmond Ryan recalled. 'Our khaki guardians came round to give us mugs and mattresses and to examine the cells; it took them the best part of a week to adjust themselves completely to the invasion.'

'What caused the riots?' the British soldiers kept asking.

'We heard early that we must shine tins, until we could see our faces therein, must fold our blankets along certain lines, keep our cells as clean as pins, listen to what the staff had to say to us, preserve the strictest military discipline with silence, not whistle or sing, not attempt to communicate with other prisoners, not to look out the windows under penalties of bread and water and an appearance before the commandant.'

After two weeks they were allowed to write home, and Collins wrote to Hannie. 'Positively you have no idea of what it's like – the dreadful monotony – the heart-scalding eternal brooding on all sorts of things, thoughts of friends dead and living – especially those recently dead – but above all the time

– the horror of the way in which it refuses to pass.' He asked her
to send him some novels and a French grammar that had been at
the flat before he left London. He found it very hard to concentrate and Oscar Wilde's 'Ballad of Reading Gaol' kept
running through his mind.

Restrictions were relaxed gradually and the authorities became 'really very benign', according to Joe Sweeney, who recalled that 'we had the life of Riley there'. The prisoners revived
their spirits with impromptu football games in the court yard,
using a makeshift ball of brown paper and rags wrapped with
twine.

'A frenzied mass of swearing, struggling, perspiring men
rolled and fought over the ball in the middle of the yard,' Ryan
recalled. 'From the din a tall, wiry, dark-haired man emerged and
his Cork accent dominated the battle for a moment. He went
under and rose and whooped and swore with tremendous vibra-
tions of his accent and then disappeared again.'

'That's Mick Collins,' someone said.

In June the prisoners were transferred to an internment camp
at Frongoch, near Barra in North Wales. Collins enjoyed the
train journey through what he described as 'the most engaging
country'. At Frongoch they joined internees from Knutsford and
other detention centres, and numbers swelled to more than
1,800 men. The camp, which had until recently housed German
prisoners-of-war was divided into two barbed wire compounds,
separated by a road. Collins, internee No. 1320, was put in the
north camp, which consisted of a series of thirty-five wooden
huts. The internees were 'given the control and management' of
the camp within the barbed wire.

Collins readily adapted himself to the conditions, and made
the most of his internment. 'He was full of fun and mischief',
remembered Batt O'Connor. 'Wherever he was, there were
always ructions and sham fights going on. Mock battles took
place between the men of his hut and the adjoining one. We had
a football field and whenever there was a game he was sure to be
in it. He was all energy and gaiety.'

Each night the men were locked up at 7.30. Between then and
lights out at 9.45 they were free to read or play cards. 'They were
listening all the time to talk and plans about the continuance of
the war as soon as we got home,' according to Batt O'Connor.
Many of the men had their own musical instruments, and they
frequently staged their own concerts and sing-songs.

Each day finished with rebel songs and recitations. Collins had a poor singing voice; so his party-piece was a forceful rendition of the poem, 'The Fighting Race' by J. I. C. Clarke. It was about three Irishmen – Kelly, Burke, and Shea, who died on the battleship *Maine* at the start of the Spanish-American war. Collins delivered the lines of all five verses with an infectious enthusiasm that made up for his inability to recite properly. The following verse gives a flavour of the poem:

> 'I wish 'twas in Ireland, for there's the place,'
>   Said Burke, 'That we'd die by right,
> In the cradle of our soldier race,
>   After one good stand-up fight.
> My grandfather fell on Vinegar Hill,
>   And fighting was not his trade;
> But his rusty pike's in the cabin still,
>   With Hessian blood on the blade.'
> 'Aye, aye,' said Kelly, 'the pikes were great
>   When the word was "clear the way!"
> We were thick on the roll in ninety-eight –
>   Kelly and Burke and Shea.'
> 'Well, here's to the pike and the sword and the like!'
>   Said Kelly and Burke and Shea.

There was plenty of time to think about what had gone wrong during Easter Week. Collins realised the strategy was faulty: it had been foolish to confront the might of Britain head on by concentrating their forces in one area. Henceforth he would learn from the mistake, but he did not believe in dwelling in the past. His attitude was best summarised in an autograph book entry he made in Frongoch.

'Let us be judged by what we attempted rather than what we achieved,' he wrote.

Each morning the men rose at 6.15. After breakfast about a quarter of them were assigned to various fatigue groups to clear out fire-places, sweep buildings, empty garbage, prepare meals, and tend a vegetable garden, etc. Those not on fatigue duty would normally go to a playing field until 11 o'clock when all the internees gathered for inspection. The commandant inspected everything in company with internee officers. The blankets on the bunks had to be folded precisely and placed on the bedboards so that they were in a straight line from one end of the room to the other, and the commandant at times used his stick to determine if the line between any two beds was not exactly straight.

The camp commandant, Colonel F. A. Heygate-Lambert, whom the internees nicknamed 'Buckshot', was a cranky, fussy individual with a lisp, always looking for something or other to complain about. 'It's hard to imagine anything in the shape of a man being more like a tyrannical old woman than the commandant in charge of this place,' Collins complained. 'The practice of confining to cells for trivial things is a thing which the commandant glories in.'

Following inspection the men were free to do much as they pleased within the camp. They played football, engaged in athletic contests, and set up classes to teach Irish, French, German, Spanish, shorthand, telegraphy, and various military skills. They drilled regularly and conducted military lectures, using manuals smuggled into the camp.

'We set up our own university there, both educational and revolutionary,' Sweeney recalled, 'and from that camp came the hard core of the subsequent guerrilla war in Ireland.' Frongoch was indeed a veritable training camp for the rebels, who acquired skills and made contacts that would prove invaluable afterwards.

'They could not have come to a better school,' Batt O'Connor wrote. 'They were thrown entirely in the company of men to whom national freedom and the old Irish traditions were the highest things in life.'

Collins and the solicitor Henry Dixon, then in his seventies, were prime movers in organising an IRB cell within the camp, and one of their recruits was Richard Mulcahy. Others in the camp who would work closely with Collins in future years, included Joe O'Reilly, Seán Hales, Gearóid O'Sullivan, J. J. 'Ginger' O'Connell, Seán Ó Muirthile, Michael Brennan, Michael Staines, Terence MacSwiney, Tomás MacCurtain, and Thomas Gay. Those were only a few of the very valuable contacts he cemented at Frongoch.

People from the camp were to be found in the forefront of Irish life throughout much of the next half century, especially in the army and police, as well as in the political arena, with a future Governor-General of the Irish Free State in Domhnall Ó Buachalla, and a future president of the Republic of Ireland in Seán T. O'Kelly, as well as future cabinet ministers in Mulcahy, O'Kelly,

Oscar Traynor, Tom Derig, Jim Ryan, and Gerry Boland.

Of course, not all of those people liked Collins personally. Many found him childish and overbearing. It was here that he earned the nickname, 'The Big Fellow'. He was not quite six feet tall and had a rather wiry, athletic build together with a youthful appearance that belied his twenty-six years, so the nickname had nothing to do with his physical characteristics. It would later become a term of affection, but it did not have its origins in affection; rather, it was a sarcastic reflection of Collins' exaggerated sense of his own importance.

Many colleagues were repulsed by his bullying tactics and his inability to concede gracefully. Being highly competitive, he hated to lose at anything. 'In the camp, if he didn't win all the jumps, he'd break up the match,' Gerry Boland recalled. When Collins had a good hand playing cards, he would concentrate intensely and would resent interruptions, but when the cards were running against him, he would renege, look into the hands of the men beside him, upset the deck and even jump on the likely winner and wrestle him to the floor.

He was fond of wrestling, or looking for 'a piece of ear'. But these wrestling bouts often ended up in real fights. He was not only a bad loser but also a bad winner. Having forced someone into submission, he would crow with delight in a high-spirited show of exuberance that more than a few found irritating.

On 8 August the internees held a sports meeting in the camp, and Collins won the 100 years dash. As he breezed past the leader, he grinned gleefully. 'Ah, you whore,' he said, 'you can't run!'

His victory was actually mentioned in the House of Commons, much to his own annoyance, because the person who raised it cited his winning time as evidence that the men were being properly fed at the camp, but this had nothing to do with camp food, as far as Collins was concerned.

'Actually there isn't a solitary man here of no matter how slender an appetite who could live on the official rations,' Collins wrote. 'There are two or three committees supplying us with additional vegetables and sometimes apples and cocoa.' It was also possible to buy extra food, but most of the men had little money. They could avail of parole to work at a nearby quarry for five-and-a-half pence an hour, but on 1 September the camp commandant announced he was deducting three pence per hour for their upkeep, and they promptly downed tools and refused to do further work. Hence the meals at the camp were important.

There were three meals each day. Both breakfast and the evening meal consisted of eight ounces of bread and almost a pint of tea, and the mid-day dinner did not show much more imagination. 'With the exception of Friday when we get uneatable herrings, the food never varies,' he wrote. 'Frozen meat, quite frequently bad, and dried beans, are the staple diets. The potato ration is so small that one hardly notices it.'

Morale was comparatively good considering the circumstances under which many of the men were interned. All of those with whom Collins had been sent to Stafford had taken part in the rebellion, but he was surprised to learn that many of the men in Frongoch played no part in the fighting. 'By my own count,' he wrote, 'at least a quarter of the men in the north camp knew very little about the Rising. One man, a former labourer of my acquaintance, said that he was just forced off the street in the round-up. His only crime appears to be that he was walking the street.'

When Prime Minister Herbert H. Asquith visited Dublin in May following the executions, he talked to some of the people being held at Richmond Barracks. 'They were mostly from remote areas of the country and none had taken any part in the Dublin Rising,' he wrote to his wife. He therefore instructed the military to comb out the prisoners properly and 'only send to England those against whom there was a real case.' By then, however, more than 1,900 prisoners had already been deported, so the British government set up a committee to examine the case against each of those being held. All of the internees were brought, in turn, before the committee in London, and a considerable number were freed.

By mid-August some 600 men had been released from Frongoch because they had taken no part in the Easter Rising. Those remaining in the north camp were then transferred to the south camp, with the north camp being retained as a punishment centre.

The south camp consisted of a disused distillery in which an abandoned granary building was converted into five large dormitories with between 150 and 250 beds in each. The beds consisted of three boards on a frame, four inches off the floor, and each man had two blankets. The low, nine-foot-high ceiling contributed to the claustrophobic atmosphere in the large rooms with so many men crammed together, and confined from 7.30 at night until 6.15 the following morning. Long before the morning the air would become quite foul, no doubt aggravated by the renowned flatulent qualities of the men's daily diet of beans.

'In some unfavoured spots, breathing is almost difficult in the morning,' Collins wrote. Luckily his bunk was beside a window and he did not suffer so much in that respect, but when it rained he could get wet as he could not close the window.

Collins had an easier time adapting himself to the conditions than many of the men, especially those married with families. He did not have to worry about a wife or children and, in any case, most of his friends were interned with him, with the result that he was never really lonely, as were many others. 'It is pitiable to see those who have given way to imprisonment now enforcing on themselves the extra burden of loneliness,' he wrote.

It was easier, of course, for him to take a more philosophical outlook. 'I'm here and that's the thing that matters,' he wrote. 'Prating about home, friends and so on doesn't alter the fact that this is Frongoch, an internment camp, and that I'm a member of the camp. There's only one thing to do while the situation is as it is – make what I can of it.'

On 3 September Hugh Thornton, one of the internees, was informed that he was liable for conscription because he had been living in Britain at the outbreak of the Great War. All told some sixty internees, including Collins, were in the same category. In Dublin before the rebellion they had been known as 'refugees', and the name stuck.

When the authorities came looking for Thornton two days later, he refused to identify himself. All the internees were forced to turn out in the yard and line up in two straight rows, but the guards were unable to recognise Thornton, and he still refused to identify himself. With the internees surrounded by a provocative array of military with loaded rifles and fixed-bayonets, the camp adjutant ordered the roll to be called. As each name was read out the man was to answer, 'Here, Sir,' and then march in front of the adjutant to the end of the yard and re-form in numerical order.

'These instructions were promptly and even cheerfully obeyed by all the prisoners,' according to themselves. By the time Thornton's number, 1,454, was called and he had answered, the camp authorities were irate.

'You have hitherto conducted the camp in an excellent manner, but this incident this morning was the worst exhibition of insubordination which I have met so far, and I cannot overlook it,' the commandant told the assembled men. As a punishment, he suspended all letters, newspapers and visits for a week.

'This harsh and unjust punishment' was resented by the internees. Many of them did not know Thornton. Michael Staines, their leader, could not have identified him 'even if he had wished to', the prisoners contended.

'Obviously everybody could not have known the particular man,' Collins wrote to Hannie. 'It is not very just to attempt to make prisoners identify a fellow prisoner,' he added. 'On the same day another man was sentenced to cells with bread and water for forgetting to say "sir" to an officer.'

On 9 September another dispute came to a head when internees on fatigue duty refused to clear refuse from the huts of guards. Prior to the start of the month this work had been contracted to an outside company, but the camp commandant decided to save money by using internees. Now they balked and, as a punishment, he ordered that they be sent to the north camp and deprived of their letters, newspapers, smoking material and visits. Each day thereafter eight more men would be transferred after they refused to do the work.

There was, of course, strict censorship at the camp but the men managed to smuggle out detailed reports to the nationalist member of parliament, Tim Healy, and Alfie Byrne of Dublin Corporation, who proceeded to publicise the whole affair, which received intensive coverage, especially in the Irish-American press.

The smuggling was done in various ways. Sometimes guards were bribed to take out letters and post them outside the camp. Another way was to have someone being released take letters out. These would be enclosed in old envelopes addressed to the person being released as if they were letters that had already been censored on entering the camp. The camp staff never detected this. Others placed letters in the sandwiches being prepared for men being released.

'The game of smuggling and communication is one for which there is no definite end,' Collins wrote to a friend. 'In its present form it could go on for ever. Daily the British grow more weary of attempting counter-action to it. As one of them remarked, "If you were bloody Jerries we'd know what to do. But you're not."'

The whole thing was really a game or a contest between the guards and internees. Collins welcomed the challenge. 'It gives some spice to the usual monotony,' he wrote.

One man who worked in the censor's office used to remove mail for Collins before the censor could read it. In this way the men established two-way communication with the outside, which was invaluable for propaganda purposes.

On 21 October the camp authorities relented and moved all the internees to the north camp, where the grass pathways quickly turned to mud amid the autumn rains. In spite of the mud, however, Collins welcomed the move back. 'Nothing could be as bad as the horrible stuffiness of the other place,' he wrote to Hannie. 'On the whole, I think the huts are better,' he added. 'In any case they're more desirable and there's a fire. There are only 29 in each now and we have a nice crowd in ours.' Some of them enjoyed reading like Collins, and they shared their books and magazines. 'Between us we haven't a bad library,' he explained.

Hugh Thornton, the 'refugee' discovered in September, had been sentenced to two years hard labour for evading conscription, with the result that while Collins was 'very active in the camp', he had to remain inconspicuous and, in order to avoid detection, he never acted as a formal spokesman.

They were always slow about identifying themselves, much to the annoyance of guards. 'Why the fuck don't ye holler out when I call yer fucking names!' exclaimed a Welsh sergeant major.

'For Christ's sake,' another exasperated guard exclaimed, 'answer to the name you go by, if you don't know your real name.'

The men naturally took delight in upsetting the guards. One morning while a count was being conducted, an internee started coughing, and the officer of the guard shouted at him to stop, whereupon all the internees began coughing.

In early November the camp authorities tricked Fintan Murphy, one of the refugees, into identifying himself by announcing that he should pick up a package, and they tried to single out Michael Murphy by saying that he was to be released as his wife was ill, but that ruse failed because Michael Murphy was not married. The commandant then tried to find him by using the same tactic used to uncover Thornton, but this time 342 men refused to answer to their names. As a punishment they were moved back to the south camp and their privileges were withdrawn. Most of the 204 men who answered the roll call on that occasion, did so by agreement in order to keep the two camps opened and thereby maintain their contact with the outside world. Fifteen of the hut leaders were court-martialled.

'The court may understand this better if I put it this way,' Richard Mulcahy explained in his defence. 'If a German interned among English soldiers by the Germans were wanted for the German army what would be thought of those English soldiers if they gave the man up and informed on him to the German authorities. There are men here who fought in the insurrection; many are here who did not; but most of them now are very sympathetic with those who did.'

A number of refugees felt badly about others suffering to protect them. They considered giving themselves up, but Collins – who was generally recognised as the leader of the refugees, would not hear of it.

'Mick burst into the meeting and sat down,' Joe O'Reilly recalled. 'When he heard their proposition he told them to do nothing of the kind but sit tight, and not to mind the cowards.'

The Easter Rebellion had taught him that Ireland was not capable of beating the British militarily, but in Frongoch he learned it was possible to beat them by wearing down their patience. 'Sit down – refuse to budge – you have the British beaten,' he wrote to a friend. 'For a time they'll raise war – in the end they'll despair.'

He was right. The British tired not only of trying to uncover the refugees, but of the whole internee problem, as it was becoming an embarrassment.

As a result of Alfie Byrne's agitation on the men's behalf Sir Charles Cameron, a retired medical officer of Dublin Corporation, visited Frongoch on 7 December along with a doctor nominated by the Home Office. The internees tried to project an image of deprivation by dressing in their worst clothes, and they complained bitterly about their food, which was actually upgraded for the occasion.

'Is there anything which you get enough of?' Cameron asked.

'Oh yes,' replied Collins, 'we get enough salt.'

Collins was clearly encouraged by the visit. 'This state of affairs can't last much longer,' he wrote next day. 'While many of the men are looking forward dismally to the prospect of spending Christmas here, I would not be surprised to find myself at home for that event.' No doubt his optimism was further encouraged by the recent political crisis which saw the fall of Asquith and the advent of a coalition government under David Lloyd George.

On 21 December the internees were summoned to the dining-hall and told they were being released. The officer on duty said, however, that he needed their names and addresses.

'It's no use,' cried Collins. 'You'll get no names and no addresses from us.'

The officer explained that he had no further interest in Michael Murphy, and did not 'give a damn' who was who, but they would have to help him if they wanted to get home by Christmas. 'I will have to telegraph the name and address of every prisoner to the Home Office and Dublin Castle before he leaves the camp,' he said. 'It will be an all night job for me unless you help. I will not be able to get through on time.'

Collins and Brennan Whitmore talked to the officer and agreed to draw up the list themselves, which solved the officer's problem. The men were then taken to Holyhead, where Collins got a boat to Kingstown, arriving back in time for Christmas, a free and wiser man.

4. 'Being Called Bad Names'

Following his release Collins went home to Clonakilty for a brief holiday but was clearly disappointed. 'From the national point of view,' he wrote to Hannie, 'I'm not too impressed with the people here. Too damn careful and cautious. A few old men aren't too bad but most of the young ones are the limit. The little bit of material prosperity has ruined them.'

After a brief stay he returned to Dublin and applied for a job as secretary of the Irish National Aid and Volunteers' Dependents' Fund, an amalgamation of two charitable organisations established following the Rebellion to help rebel prisoners and their families. One had been set by Dublin Corporation and the other by Tom Clarke's widow, Kathleen, who used gold left over from what Clan na Gael had provided to finance the Rebellion. Collins did not realise that some friends from Frongoch pulled strings for him to get the job.

'We worked like hell, though we were careful to keep any knowledge from him of what we were doing,' one of them recalled. 'Mick would have taken a very sour view of our part in the affair.'

Collins realised that there was resistance to his appointment. 'I was regarded with a certain amount of suspicion,' he wrote to a friend. 'I was young and would therefore be almost certain to be irresponsible to the importance of the position.' He thought his involvement in the Rebellion was frowned upon by the committee, especially the ladies. 'In the end,' he wrote, 'chiefly by good fortune the job became mine.'

In his new position he was in contact with a wide spectrum of people sympathetic to the separatist movement. Kathleen Clarke provided him with the names of IRB contacts throughout the country. As his work was of a charitable nature he was able to travel widely without rousing the slightest suspicion. With the recognised leaders still in jail, he became particularly influential in rebuilding the IRB. He took an active part and 'had a great time' in Count Plunkett's campaign for a vacant parliamentary seat in Roscommon.

From the outset Collins was optimistic. 'Consider the situation,' he wrote on 19 January 1917. 'It is ripe for whatever one may wish.' He believed the Irish Parliamentary Party and the Crown authorities were now 'in a corner, driven there by what they have done and by the will of the people.'

'The crowds were splendid,' he wrote to Hannie. 'It was really pleasing to see so many old lads coming out in the snow and voting for Plunkett with the greatest enthusiasm. Practically all the very old people were solid for us and on the other end the young ones.' Plunkett won the seat, and in the process provided a tremendous boost for the separatist movement.

The work of reorganising the IRB took up a lot of Collins' time because there was so much to be done. 'It is only since being released that I'm feeling to the full all that we have lost in the way of men and workers,' he noted. As a result he was 'kept going from morning till night and usually into the next morning'. He was suspicious of some of the people who were offering help. 'I haven't the prevailing belief in the many conversions to our cause' and he wrote that he 'incurred a good deal of unpopularity through telling people so'.

The separatist movement really consisted of a number of different organisations, each with its own leader. Arthur Griffith was the head of Sinn Féin, Count Plunkett of the Liberty League, Eoin MacNeill was still nominally the head of the Irish Volunteers, and Thomas Ashe had been elected head of the IRB. In addition, there was Eamon de Valera, the elected spokesman of the prisoners in Lewes Jail. He had nominally been a member of the IRB, but had never been really active in the organisation, because he had an orthodox Catholic dislike for oath-bound societies.

De Valera owed his prominence to two factors. Firstly, men fighting under his command had inflicted the heaviest casualties on the British army during the Easter Rising. And secondly, he was not too closely identified with any of the various organisations. He came to prominence at Lewes one morning when – noticing MacNeill coming down stairs – he called the other rebel prisoners to attention to salute their chief-of-staff. Although many of the men despised MacNeill for countermanding the orders for the Rebellion, they heeded de Valera's call rather than show disunity in front of their British jailers. No matter what they thought of MacNeill personally, he was still an Irishman and a fellow prisoner; if only on those grounds alone, they would respect him. De Valera's gesture towards MacNeill was probably more responsible than anything else for his election as spokesman for the prisoners.

Collins made secret contact with Ashe in Lewes Jail, where he was serving a life sentence for his part in the Easter Rising. He had been defeated by de Valera for the leadership of the Irish prisoners in the jail. When a parliamentary by-election was called in Longford for April, Collins wrote to Ashe about nominating Joe McGuinness, one of the Lewes prisoners who was from the Longford area.

It was only with difficulty that Arthur Griffith had been persuaded not to put forward a Sinn Féin candidate who would split the vote. Consequently Collins resented it when some IRB people were critical of his attempt to run McGuinness. 'If you only knew of the long fights I've had with A. G[riffith] and some of his pals before I could gain the present point,' Collins wrote. 'The difference we had with him in the old school has been continued and grows more intense according as the new school passes into working order.'

Although Griffith had played no part in the Easter Rising and was, in fact, opposed to it, the Rebellion was nevertheless widely identified with his party in the public mind, because Sinn Féin had been in the vanguard of the separatist movement for more than a decade.

'It is rather disgusting to be "chalked up" as a follower of his,' Collins wrote to Ashe.

At this period he tended to express his views with a harshness that was often unattractive. While Griffiths wanted full independence for Ireland, he was not a Republican. Instead he advocated an Anglo-Irish dual monarchy on Austro-Hungarian lines, and he believed it could be achieved by non-violent means. Collins, on the other hand, was 'the very incarnation of out-and-out physical force Republicanism.'

'This Sinn Féin stunt is a bloody balderdash!' Collins snapped at one meeting. 'We want a Republic!'

Griffith stared at him, and Collins became uneasy. 'Of course,' he added, 'I don't know much about Sinn Féin.'

'Evidently not, Mr Collins, or you wouldn't talk like you do,' replied Griffith.

Of course, Collins knew full well what Sinn Féin stood for. He had admired Griffith as a boy and had been active in the party himself during his early years in London. While he no longer shared Griffith's more moderate views, he still thought enough of him to try to excuse his rash remark. A stubborn, opinionated politician with a resolute determination, Griffith was a fanatic in his own right, but he was unselfish in his dedication to the separatist cause. Hence he agreed not to put up a Sinn Féin candidate against McGuinness in order that the release of all the remaining prisoners who had taken part in the Rebellion could be made an election issue. Ashe liked the idea, but de Valera was opposed and managed to persuade McGuinness to decline the invitation.

As the by-election was likely to be closely contested, de Valera felt the movement's morale would be irreparably damaged by defeat at the polls, but Collins was not about to stand for such timidity. Ignoring his instructions from Lewes Jail, he had McGuinness' name put forward anyway, much to the annoyance of IRB people in Lewes like Seán McGarry and Con Collins who had sided with de Valera against Ashe on the issue.

'You can tell Con Collins, Seán McGarry and any other highbrows that I have been getting all their scathing messages, and am not a little annoyed, or at least was, but one gets so used to being called bad names and being misunderstood.'

His judgment was vindicated when McGuinness was elected on the slogan: 'Put him in to get him out.'

The victory helped to increase pressure on the Lloyd George government to release the remaining prisoners. All were freed on 17 June 1917, and returned to a hero's welcome in Dublin next day. It was little over a year since they had been deported in disgrace, both despised and dispirited. Collins, who helped organise the welcoming reception, was the model of efficiency. He had worked out the travel costs of all the released prisoners from Dublin to their homes, but his rather abrupt, businesslike manner was a little too officious for some.

Robert Brennan, one of those released from Lewes, had already noticed the pale, fast-moving, energetic young man darting here and there. He was all business. He frequently dispensed with formalities like shaking hands or even saying good morning. He came over and, without bothering to introduce himself, said Brennan was to look after those returning to Wexford.

'He had a role of notes in one hand and silver in the other,' Brennan recalled. 'He said that the fares to Enniscorthy amounted to so much, and I found out later the sum was correct to a penny. He added that he was giving me five shillings, in addition, for each man, to cover incidental expenses. As he handed me the money, he looked into my eyes as if appraising me. With a quick smile, he shook my hand and turned to someone else.'

'Who is he?' Brennan asked a colleague.

'Michael Collins,' the friend replied.

'I don't like him,' said Brennan.

As the elected spokesman of the returning prisoners de Valera immediately gained public prominence. A by-election had been called for East Clare the following month and he was selected to contest the seat.

On making his first appearance on an election platform in Ennis, he was careful to include Eoin MacNeill on the platform. In the process he won the reputation as unifying force, and he exploited the situation with considerable political finesse. By associating himself with MacNeill – who was despised by radical militants like Collins – he acquired a reputation as a moderate, which was important because MacNeill was representative of a majority of those supporting the party; most had not taken part in the fighting, and with someone like him at the forefront they would not feel like second class supporters. At the same time, however, de Valera was careful to appeal to the more militant elements by evoking the spirit of 1916 in his election addresses.

Indeed, he talked so much about the Rebellion that some myths would gradually grow around his own role in the fighting. It would be said, and widely believed, that he was the last commandant to surrender and the only one to survive the subsequent executions, but neither assertion was true. Two other commandants survived, Thomas Hunter and Thomas Ashe, and the latter had actually been the last to surrender.

De Valera was easily elected, as was W. T. Cosgrave in a Kilkenny by-election the following month. Speaking at an election rally in Kilkenny on 5 August, de Valera declared that they would fight England first with ballots, and if that failed, they would fight with rifles.

In August Ashe was arrested and charged with making a seditious speech in Ballinalee, where it so happened that Collins had shared the platform with him. While Ashe was in custody, Collins visited him in the Curragh detention centre and attended his court-martial a fortnight later. 'The whole business was extremely entertaining, almost as good a Gilbert and Sullivan skit trial by jury,' Collins wrote to Ashe's sister immediately afterwards.

'The President of the Court was obviously biased against Tom, and, although the charge is very trivial, and the witnesses contradicted each other, it is quite likely that Tom will be sentenced.'

Ashe was duly sentenced to a prison term, as expected. He demanded prisoner-of-war status and when this was refused, he went on hunger-strike. The authorities decided to feed him forcibly and he died on 25 September as a result of injuries received in the process. His death was to have a tremendous impact on public opinion, especially on young people. Some later argued that Ashe's death had greater effect on the country than even the Easter Rising.

Collins was particularly upset. 'I grieve perhaps as no one else grieves,' he wrote. Dressed in the uniform of a vice-commandant, he delivered the grave-side address, which was stirring in its simplicity. 'Nothing additional remains to be said,' he declared following the sounding of the last post and the firing of a volley of shots. 'That volley which we have just heard is the only speech which it is proper to make over the grave of a dead Fenian.'

On 8 October Collins went back to speak in Ballinalee. 'In the circumstances,' he noted, 'I came out on the strong side'. All went well except that there was 'a bit of unpleasantness with a policeman who was taking notes'. When confronted the policeman thought it best to surrender those notes, and there was no further problem.

Without a recognised leader of its own, the IRB supported de Valera when the various separatist organisations came together under the Sinn Féin banner on 25 October. He was the obvious choice because he had been a member of the IRB and was not closely associated with any of the political organisations. In addition his record during the Easter Rebellion as the commandant whose men inflicted most casualties on the British made him a symbol for Republican militants, and he played on the militancy of people like Collins.

'England pretends it is not here by the naked sword, but by the good-will of the people of the country that she is here,' de Valera told the Ard Fheis. 'We will draw the naked sword to make her bare her own naked sword.'

Griffith and Plunkett withdrew their own nominations for the Presidency of the newly united party in favour of de Valera, who was duly elected by acclamation. Griffith was then elected

Vice-President along with Father Michael O'Flanagan, while Count Plunkett and Austin Stack, an IRB activist, were elected Joint Honorary Secretary.

Collins campaigned enthusiastically for de Valera, and gave members of the IRB a list of twenty-four people to be supported for the party Executive, for which he was standing himself. Most of those on his list were defeated, and to add insult to injury, MacNeill headed the poll with 888 votes, while Collins and IRB colleague, Ernest Blythe, tied for the last two places with 340 votes each.

Next day de Valera was also elected President of the Irish Volunteers at a separate convention, again with the enthusiastic support of Collins and the IRB. This time Collins was appointed Director of Organisation of the Volunteers.

A twenty-six-man executive was established with a small 'resident executive' to oversee the day-to-day running of the Volunteers. Cathal Brugha was put in charge of the Executive, but things were a little too loose, so it was decided to set up a headquarters' staff. Seven of the most prominent members of the resident executive met at the headquarters of the printer's union at 35 Lower Gardiner Street to select a Chief-of-Staff in March 1918. Those attending were Collins, Mulcahy, Dick McKee, Gearóid O'Sullivan, Diarmuid O'Hegarty, Rory O'Connor, and Seán McMahon.

They discussed the matter and even those close to Collins were 'wary of entrusting him with anything like complete control'. They clearly had doubts about his volatile temperament, and they looked to Mulcahy instead.

'We agreed among ourselves,' Mulcahy wrote, 'that I would become Chief-of-Staff.' Collins was appointed Adjutant General instead, in addition to his post as Director of Organisation.

As Adjutant General he was in charge of training and inculcating discipline. He therefore travelled about the country reorganising the force, and speaking to various meetings, despite harassment by the police. On 2 April 1918 he was arrested in Dublin for a speech that he had made in Longford some days earlier. He was bound over for a further hearing in July. On refusing to post bail he was transferred to Sligo Jail.

'Before me therefore is the prospect of a prolonged holiday and of course July will only be the real commencement of it,' he wrote to Hannie. He had 'hardly anyone to talk to' in Sligo, so he did a good deal of reading and study, especially Irish history and the Irish language. He also tried to follow the political crisis brewing as the British government mulled over the possibility of introducing conscription in Ireland.

'I'm very anxious to know what Lloyd George has done about conscription for this country,' Collins wrote on 10 April. 'If he goes for it – well he's ended'. In fact, the British government had already introduced a bill the previous day to enable it to extend conscription to Ireland. The bill was rushed through parliament, and the Irish Parliamentary Party (IPP) walked out of Westminster in protest.

This was another major turning point for the independence movement. Although separatists had enjoyed four consecutive by-election victories in 1917, they seemed to run out of steam after they came together under the Sinn Féin banner because the party lost the next three by-elections to the IPP in the following months.

However, the IPP was damaged irreparably by the conscription crisis; its withdrawal from Westminster in protest against the new act was tantamount to endorsing the abstentionist policy advocated all along by Sinn Féin.

Collins quickly realised the implications of what was happening. 'The conscription proposals are to my liking as I think they will end well for Ireland,' he wrote. The controversy afforded a tremendous opportunity for Sinn Féin to exploit public resentment. He duly posted bail to take part in a massive anti-conscription campaign being orchestrated by Sinn Féin .

A conference of the different Irish nationalist groups was held in Dublin at the Mansion House on 18 April, and it issued a declaration that bore the indelible imprint of separatist thinking by basing the case against conscription on 'Ireland's separate and distinct nationhood' and denying 'the right of the British government, or any external authority, to impose compulsory service in Ireland against the clearly expressed will of the Irish people.'

De Valera persuaded the conference to enlist the support of the Catholic hierarchy, which virtually sanctified the campaign against conscription by ordering that a special Mass be said the following Sunday 'in every church in Ireland to avert the scourge of conscription with which Ireland is now threatened'. With the country in uproar, the British dared not implement the bill, but did try to remove Sinn Féin from the scene on the night of 18 May by rounding up the leadership for supposedly being involved in a plot with Germany against Britain.

Joe Kavanagh, a police detective, gave Thomas Gay, a public librarian, a list of those to be arrested that night. Gay, a former colleague in Frongoch, passed the list on to Collins, who had already received a warning from a different source. Two days earlier a friend had been tipped off by another detective, Ned Broy, though the latter had not been able to mention any specific names at the time.

It so happened that the Sinn Féin executive was meeting on the evening of 18 May at its headquarters in 6 Harcourt Street. The leaders decided the best course was to let the Crown authorities arrest them as there was another by-election coming up in East Cavan, and they felt that their arrest would enhance Arthur Griffith's chances of winning the seat and stopping the rot of the recent reversals. The leaders felt there were enough energetic young men around to keep the movement going.

Afterwards Collins went to warn Seán McGarry, the President of the IRB, but his home was already in the process of being raided so Collins joined with the curious onlookers as McGarry was taken away. He then spent the night in McGarry's home as it was unlikely to be raided again that night.

No convincing evidence of a German Plot was produced and certainly the arrested leaders of Sinn Féin, like de Valera, Griffith, Plunkett, McGuinness, Cosgrave and MacNeill were not involved. People inevitably concluded that the arrests were really designed to undermine the anti-conscription campaign of Sinn Féin, which was therefore able to make enormous political capital out of the arrests. The popular urge to fight conscription was a great impetus to enlistment in the Volunteers. Popular feelings were so strong in Ireland that the Westminster government announced on 3 June that conscription could be postponed until October, at least. As the IPP had been unable to prevent the passage of the bill in the first place, Sinn Féin was given the credit for forcing the government to back down, and Griffith won the by-election easily three weeks later.

With the easing of the crisis there was a distinct decline in the membership of the Volunteers, but many new recruits had still been gained. An even more far-reaching consequence of the crisis was the vacuum left at the top of the movement by the arrest of moderates like de Valera, Griffith, and MacNeill, who had been exerting a restraining influence. They had designated replacements within the party but those people lacked the stature to keep militants like Collins and Cathal Brugha in line. The militants suddenly had more influence than ever, and they were gradually able to exert a kind of ascendancy of their own.

On 5 July the British government banned all public gatherings such as football matches and political rallies without a police permit, and Sinn Féin set about defying the ban. The GAA held football and hurling matches throughout the country in open defiance on 4 August, and on Assumption Thursday, eleven days later, Sinn Féin held some 1,800 public rallies throughout the country in mass defiance of the government.

With so many prominent members of the movement in jail Collins set about organising a network to smuggle letters in and out of jail. Calling on his own experience from Frongoch, he enlisted the help of certain guards and visitors to the prisons to carry messages for him.

Although a member of the Sinn Féin Executive, Collins concentrated on organisational matters within the Volunteers and was largely contemptuous of politicians. And he felt that Sinn Féin, in particular, lacked direction. Executive meetings were poorly attended, and the discussions 'lacked any great force,' according to him. He was particularly critical of Sinn Féin Vice-President Father Michael O'Flanagan for 'hob nobbing' with Crown officials, or the 'enemy,' as Collins saw it.

Collins was looking for action, not talk. His views were best represented in an article written for *An t-Óglach* by Ernest Blythe, a northern Protestant who had adopted the nationalist cause with all the zeal of a radical convert. 'We must recognise,' Blythe wrote, 'that anyone, civilian or soldier, who assists directly or by convenience in this crime against us, merits no more consideration than a wild beast, and should be killed without mercy or hesitation as opportunity offers.'

As Director of Organisation, Collins was deeply involved with the publication of *An t-Óglach*. He wrote the column, 'Notes on Organisation,' and also directed and distributed the publication personally. He was so taken with Blythe's article, that he asked for more of the same from him.

With de Valera and Griffith in jail, O'Flanagan was nominally in charge of Sinn Féin, and he presided at meetings of the executive. Collins still had little time for the clergy, and he had even less for that political priest and the people around him. They did too much talking and not enough work, while Collins was all action.

When he wanted things done, he wanted them done immediately, with no excuses. 'Have you got it?' he would ask. 'If you haven't got it, don't mind the excuses, but go and get it.'

'There are one hundred copies of the September number of *An t-Óglach* allotted to your brigade, so the amount due is 16/8, please forward this sum without delay,' he wrote to Michael de Lacy in Limerick on 31 August 1918. 'By attending to this at once you will greatly facilitate matters.' In the next ten days he impatiently sent two more reminders, and when he still had not received the money after a fortnight, he despatched a demand. 'I do not request,' Collins wrote. 'I insist.'

When Ernie O'Malley met him in his office at Bachelor's Walk, he found Collins pacing up and down impatiently. 'He jerked his head to a chair to indicate I should sit,' O'Malley noted. 'He took a chair which he tilted back against the wall. It was an awkward gesture, not an indication of relaxation because Collins was not relaxed. Instead he projected an image of frustrated restraint with energy exuding in his rapid gestures. A lock of hair would fall down over his forehead, and he would toss it back with a vigorous twist of his head. His tilted chair was an unconscious display of arrogance. This was the Big Fellow showing off. At one point he mentioned a recent raid in which Inspector Bruton of the DMP found empty packing cases and ammunition wrappers.'

'This looks as if there were brains behind it,' Collins quoted the inspector as supposedly having said. 'I bet it's that fellow from Mountjoy Street.' At the time Collins was living in the Munster Hotel at 44 Mountjoy Street. He was trying to impress O'Malley, and, of course, he was trying too hard. His display of raw vanity had the opposite effect. O'Malley formed an instinctive dislike which he was never quite able to overcome.

Probably the best insight into Collins' thinking around this time can be leaned from his correspondence with Stack. The latter had been close to Ashe, a fellow Kerryman, and this probably prompted Collins to hold him in extremely high regard, though they could hardly have known each other very well at the time. Yet Collins wrote to him in effusive terms, informing him of happenings on the outside and seeking his advice.

'I was very glad to get your letter, especially the personal note which I appreciated,' Collins wrote to him on 29 August. 'Without insincerity I can say that I do appreciate it more from yourself than from anyone I know.' It was ironic that they would become the bitterest of political enemies in the days ahead.

5. 'Too Many of the Bargaining Type'

While the signing of the armistice ending the Great War was warmly welcomed throughout the British Empire, there were some ugly incidents in Dublin when a large crowd gathered to celebrate. Collins was attending a staff meeting of the Volunteers at the time so he was not involved, but he seemed to take a vicarious delight in writing about attacks made on soldiers.

'As a result of various encounters there were 125 cases of wounded soldiers treated at Dublin hospitals that night', he wrote to Austin Stack. 'Before morning 3 soldiers and 1 officer had ceased to need any attention and one other died the following day. A policeman too was in a precarious condition up to a few days ago when I ceased to take any further interest in him. He was unlikely to recover.'

This was Collins at his least attractive. While in Frongoch he had asked that those who had taken part in the Easter Rebellion should be judged by what they attempted rather than what they achieved, yet he was unwilling to judge the soldiers who had fought in the Great War by the same standard.

Those who had answered John Redmond's call to battle had undoubtedly believed they were acting in Ireland's best interest. Some 200,000 Irishmen fought, most voluntarily, and some 50,000 lost their lives. Against those figures the number of Irishmen who fought or died in the War of Independence, paled into relative insignificance. Some like Tom Barry and Emmet Dalton returned home from the Great War to fight against the Crown in the independence struggle.

Instead of alienating the war veterans with their thuggery on Armistice Day, separatist supporters would have been better served if they had tried to enlist those people in the cause. What the veterans had tried to do was scoffed at by Sinn Féin, and then betrayed by Lloyd George and his government, which was prepared to sacrifice anything and virtually everything for short-term political gain.

The wily Welshman sought to exploit public emotions by promising to squeeze Germany until the pips squeak. In the process he, and his like, prepared the ground on which Adolf Hitler and the Nazis would thrive. Britain would pay dearly for the selfish, calculating policies of Lloyd George in the coming years. Indeed she would come perilously close to losing all in the summer of 1940.

When Lloyd George sought to capitalise on the emotions that greeted the end of the war by calling a general election, Sinn Féin put up candidates throughout the country. With so many leaders in jail as a result of the so-called German Plot, Collins played a large part in the campaign. Together with Harry Boland and Diarmuid O'Hegarty, he was primarily responsible for the selection of Sinn Féin candidates. Such was the extent of the backstage management of the party's campaign that many of the candidates – most of whom were in jail – did not even know their names were being put forward.

As far as Collins was concerned the whole thing was a necessary propaganda exercise in which he played a very active though somewhat reluctant part. He would have obviously preferred to have been able to devote more time to preparations to spring Stack from Belfast Jail, where he was recently transferred. 'Damn these elections,' he exclaimed in a letter to Stack in the midst of the campaign.

His own election address to the voters of Cork was brief and to the point: 'You are requested by your votes, to assert before the nations of the world that Ireland's claim is to the status of an independent nation, and that we shall be satisfied with nothing less than our full claim – that in fact, any scheme of government which does not confer upon the people of Ireland the supreme, absolute, and final control of all this country, external as well as internal, is a mockery and will not be accepted.'

Sinn Féin enjoyed a magnificent victory at the polls, winning 73 seats against 26 for the Unionist Party and only 6 for the once powerful IPP. It was a case of organisational brilliance of which there are few parallels. The party claimed a clear mandate for its platform to establish an Irish Republic with its own sovereign assembly in Ireland.

On 7 January 1919 Collins was among twenty-four victorious Sinn Féin candidates who met to consider their next move. At the outset they took the following oath:

I hereby pledge myself to work for the establishment of an independent Irish Republic; that I will accept nothing less than complete separation from England in settlement of Ireland's claims; and that I will abstain from attending the English Parliament.

The meeting proceeded to discuss arrangements to set up the promised national assembly, Dáil Éireann. Collins wrote that he was 'very much against' this while so many elected representatives were in jail. And it was significant that he was not present in the Mansion House on 21 January when the Dáil formally met for the first time. He felt he had better things to do.

He was later accused of being behind an ambush that day at Soloheadbeg, Country Tipperary, in which two policemen were killed while escorting a consignment of explosives being delivered to a mine. The attack, which has generally been seen as the start of the Anglo-Irish War, had been organised by Dan Breen, and Collins had no involvement whatever. In fact, he was not even in the country. He was in England at the time personally supervising the final arrangements to spring de Valera, McGarry and Séan Milroy from Lincoln Jail.

The prisoners had managed to send out a drawing of a master key, and Collins had three separate keys made; two were smuggled into the jail, but neither worked. He then had a suitable blank key delivered, along with cutting material, to enable one of the prisoners to fashion a key inside the prison. Collins made arrangements to collect the three men outside the jail and spirit them to hiding places in England, where they would wait until he could arrange their safe passage back to Ireland.

The night of 3 February was chosen for the escape attempt. While Paddy O'Donoghue waited in a taxi, Collins and Harry Boland approached the jail from a nearby field and gave a pre-arranged signal with a flashlight indicating everything was ready. Milroy responded in the jail by setting light to a whole box of matches at his cell window.

Collins tried to open a side gate with one of the keys he had made, but it jammed. With characteristic impetuosity, he tried to force it, only to have the head of the key snap off in the lock. By this time he could hear de Valera and the others approaching the other side of the gate.

'Dev,' he exclaimed, 'the key's broken in the lock!'

Fortunately de Valera managed to knock the broken piece out

with his own key. The three prisoners then emerged, to the immense relief of those outside. Collins gave de Valera a jubilant thump on the shoulder, and they all made for the taxi, which took them to the city centre. Collins and Boland got off there and took a train to London, while the three escapees changed cars and set off for the Manchester area, where they went into hiding.

With the success of the escape Collins was hoping for a military confrontation with the British. 'As for us on the outside,' Collins wrote to Stack the following week, 'all ordinary peaceful means are ended and we shall be taking the only alternative actions in a short while now.'

The independence movement was entering a new phase. He had played a major role in the re-organisation that would now allow the movement to take up the armed struggle from where it had been left off in 1916, but his role should not be over-emphasised.

Still in his late twenties he was a determined, opinionated young man, capable of making fast decisions with all the confidence of youth, but his determination was blended with an arrogance that made him intolerant of views differing from his own. In his desire for action he often failed to realise the signficance of symbolic events such as the Proclamation of the Republic by Pearse, or the establishment of Dáil Éireann, or even the importance which de Valera placed on keeping people like MacNeill within the movement. There can be no doubt that 'the Big Fellow' would not have been able to unite Sinn Féin in 1917 as de Valera had done.

Collins recognised de Valera's leadership qualities and looked to him to lead the renewed struggle. After all in his presidential address at the Sinn Féin Ard Fheis he had promised to 'draw the naked sword' in order to make the British do likewise. But when de Valera was spirited back to Ireland after a fortnight in hiding in Britain, he had no intention of renewing the armed struggle, at least not for the time being. He thought Ireland's best chance of success lay in enlisting American help in view of President Woodrow Wilson's eloquent pronouncements about the rights of small nations for which Americans had supposedly gone to war in 1917. Collins tried but failed to persuade de Valera to stay at home and direct the forthcoming struggle.

'You know what it is to argue with Dev,' Collins told a friend. 'He says he thought it out while in prison, and he feels that the one place where he can be useful to Ireland is in America.'

Collins made arrangements through his shipping contacts for the journey to the United States, and de Valera returned to Britain, where he was to be smuggled on board an American-bound ship. But while he was waiting the British government suddenly released all the German Plot prisoners, with the result that he was free to return openly to Ireland. His impending return was announced and a civic reception arranged to welcome him. He would be met at the boat and given the kind of reception normally reserved for royalty.

'The Lord Mayor of Dublin will receive him at the gates of the city, and will escort him to the Mansion House, where he will deliver a message to the Irish people,' Sinn Féin announced. But this was all too much for the British authorities, and they banned the reception.

The party was suddenly faced with a dilemma. Going ahead with the announced plans would undoubtedly lead to trouble, while abandoning them could have disastrous implications for the morale of the whole movement. Parallels were drawn with the disastrous consequences of Daniel O'Connell's buckling under similar British pressure at Clontarf some seventy years earlier.

The Sinn Féin Executive held an emergency meeting to discuss the situation. Tom Kelly, one of the National Secretaries under whose names the welcoming preparations had been published, announced that he never even saw much less signed the statement issued to the press. Collins admitted that he had written the announcement and signed Kelly's and Harry Boland's names himself. Speaking 'with vehemence and emphasis,' he made it clear that he was looking for a confrontation with the British.

'Ireland was likely to get more out of a general state of disorder than from a continuance of the situation as it then stood,' he declared, according to one of those present. 'The proper people to take decisions of that kind were ready to face the British military, and were resolved to force the issue. And they were not to be deterred by weaklings or cowards.'

A heated argument ensued, which was hardly surprising in view of the contemptuous arrogance of Collins, essentially insinuating that he had a right to commit the party to any course of action he wished. The argument was only resolved by deciding to consult de Valera, who duly asked that the welcoming demonstrations be cancelled rather than risk a confrontation in which lives might be lost. He was sure matters of much greater principle would arise in future.

'We who have waited,' he wrote to the executive, 'know how to wait. Many a heavy fish is caught even with a fine line if the angler is patient.'

Whatever harm Collins had done to his own standing by his arrogant display was more than offset by his success in organising two further prison breaks before the end of the month. The first, was the escape of Robert Barton from Mountjoy Jail on 16 March. He escaped after cutting through a window-bar with a blade provided by Collins, who had arranged for a rope to be thrown over the perimeter wall on a given signal from Barton, who used the rope to pull over a rope-ladder with which he scaled the wall. Barton was taken immediately to Batt O'Connor's house, where Collins was waiting.

'That's only the beginning,' a jubilant Collins told O'Connor.

This escape was like a trial run for a more ambitious break set for the afternoon of 29 March. The plan was to spring Pádraic Fleming and Piaras Beaslaí and whoever else could get out with them. Everything went according to plan. Volunteers, led by Rory O'Connor, threw a rope over the wall with a rope-ladder attached as they had done in the case of Barton's escape. Some prisoners overpowered the guards within the yard while the others scaled the wall. The whole thing went off better than anyone had hoped, and twenty Volunteers escaped. Having observed the escape Joe O'Reilly peddled off furiously on his bicycle to the Wicklow Hotel, where Collins was waiting impatiently.

'Is Fleming out?' he asked.

'The whole jail is out.'

'What! How many?'

'About twenty when I came away.'

Every so often as Collins sat in his office at Cullenswood House that evening, he would put down his pen and burst out laughing. They had brought off a major coup, which boosted party morale and more than off-set whatever damage had been done by the cancellation of the welcoming demonstration for de Valera.

The Dáil met on 1 April 1919 and de Valera was elected *Priomh Aire*. Next day he named a cabinet, representative of the various shades of opinion within Sinn Féin. It included Griffith, Plunkett, MacNeill, Brugha, Cosgrave, Barton, Countess Markievicz, and Collins, who was appointed Minister for Finance because he had banking experience before the Easter Rising.

The over-all occasion afforded enormous publicity for the Dáil, and Collins – despite his dislike of formal occasions – sensed something momentous about the proceedings. 'The week which has passed has been a busy one for us – perhaps it has been an historical one for very often we are actors in events that have very much more meaning and consequence than we realise,' he wrote to his sister Lena, who was a nun in England. 'Last week did, I feel, mark the inception of something new. The elected representatives of the people have definitely turned their backs on the old order and the developments are sure to be interesting. Generally the situation is working out to the satisfaction of Ireland – that is in foreign countries. At home we go from success to success in our own guerrilla way.'

'It is a most interesting thing to watch from day to day the downfall of the stern government regime,' he wrote. 'Not indeed that it is ended, not even that it won't flash forth occasionally again, but the impotence of the military governors is gradually taking them into a position which is almost chaotic. Certain it is that we are fast reaching the breaking-point.' 'Whether we achieve our object or whether we fail gloriously,' he believed, 'a mark has been made that can never be effaced.' He was rather melodramatic about his own appointment as Minister for Finance which, he told his sister, would 'simply ensure the hanging that was only probable had we remained merely members of the Dáil.'

He expected great things of de Valera, now that the latter had taken over the leadership from Fr O'Flanagan. De Valera privately expressed antipathy towards conventional politics in conversations with people like Collins and Mulcahy.

'You're a young man going into politics,' he told Mulcahy about this time. 'I'll give you two pieces of advice, study economics and read *The Prince*.' The latter book, of course, was Machiavelli's classical study of political duplicity. Mulcahy would later come to appreciate the advice, at least as a key to understanding de Valera himself.

In the following weeks Collins would become somewhat exasperated with de Valera's style of government, which was to allow endless debate and to give a much greater role to the politicians within the movement. A special Sinn Féin Ard Fheis was held on 8 April at which a proposal by de Valera was adopted, debarring members of the cabinet from membership of the party's Standing Committee, which was now given a voice in government action.

De Valera undoubtedly had Collins in mind when he explained the Standing Committee's consultative role. He said, for example, if a minister decided that the Irish people should no longer pay income tax to the Crown, the proposal would first be referred to the Standing Committee, and the proposal would be dropped if it demurred.

Collins had been arguing in favour of just such a scheme within the cabinet, but he had come up against the resolute obstinacy of Brugha. De Valera, as was his wont, had assumed an aloof position in the dispute, but his remarks at the Ard Fheis certainly leaned towards Brugha's more cautious position on the issue. The proposal giving the Standing Committee a role in government action was passed unanimously by the Ard Fheis.

Once de Valera made up his own mind on any matter he was virtually impossible to shift, though he was usually prepared to allow others to make futile efforts to dissuade him on some point or other. Of course, sitting through such arguments required an equal amount of patience on the part of other cabinet members, and this kind of patience was not one of Collins' strong points.

As Minister for Finance he had to organise funds for the independence struggle, and he did so with charateristic thoroughness. The Dáil agreed to float the National Loan by selling bonds as the Fenians had done, and Collins drafted a prospectus for the loan, but not without some problems. He was irritated by de Valera's habit of considering and weighing virtually every word carefully on the notional scale of history before agreeing to it. Collins, too, was mindful of history, but he sought a definite historical link, not just mere words. He wanted the Dáil to honour the Fenian bonds, but de Valera forced him to delete a reference to those from the prospectus.

De Valera also agonised over the wording of the Irish submission to the Paris Peace Conference. 'The damned Peace Conference will be over before he's satisfied,' Collins grumbled in frustration.

In April Collins and three colleagues went over to London in the hope of explaining the Irish situation to Woodrow Wilson on his way to the Paris Peace Conference, but the American President was unwilling to meet them. Collins was so annoyed that he suggested kidnapping the President to make him listen. Fortunately nobody took the suggestion too seriously. The proposal provided an insight into why some of his friends thought he was inclined to allow his enthusiasm to get the better of his judgment.

President Wilson obviously had no interest in the Irish case, and there was no chance of getting a meaningful hearing in Paris without his help, so Collins thought that agonising over the text of the submission to the Peace Conference was a waste of time. A deputation of three prominent Irish-Americans visited Paris in an unsuccessful bid to get Wilson to support Irish claims, and they visited Dublin in early May. The Dáil held a special public session at the Mansion House in their honour. Collins was in the building when detectives – backed up by five lorry loads of troops, a small armoured car and machine guns – raided it looking for him and a couple of other wanted men who were known to be there.

'They surrounded the building with great attention to every military detail,' Collins wrote. 'They entered the Mansion House and searched it with great care and thoroughness but they got nobody inside. The wanted ones codded them again.' Collins and the other two had slipped out of a back window and hid in an adjoining building. When the military left Collins returned, this time dressed in his Volunteers uniform; it was a show of bravado that went down well with most of the gathering, though some felt that the Big Fellow was showing off again.

'By this time everybody should know that it is by naked force that England holds this country,' Collins wrote with obvious satisfaction. 'Our American friends got an exhibition of the truth while they were here.'

Collins encouraged local units of the IVF to raid police barracks for arms. This, in addition to offering the possibility of acquiring much needed weapons, had the advantage of giving the Volunteers something to do that required organisation. It soon led to the withdrawal of the Royal Irish Constabulary from isolated areas and the abandonment of literally hundreds of police barracks throughout the country.

He was impatient for a fight. Desmond Ryan recalled an incident at Cullenswood House one day when Collins picked up an old copy of *An Cleidheam Soluis* in which Pearse had extolled the virtues of armed conflict. 'We must accustom ourselves to the thought of arms, to the sight of arms, to the use of arms,' Collins read aloud with enthusiasm. 'We may make mistakes in the beginning and shoot the wrong people, but bloodshed is a cleansing and sanctifying thing, and the nation which regards it as the final horror has lost its manhood. There are things more horrible than bloodshed; and slavery is one of them.' With that Collins slammed down the paper and walked out. No matter what he thought of Pearse at the GPO, those were his own sentiments now.

'When you asked me for ammunition for guns which have never fired a shot in this fight, my answer is a simple one,' he wrote to a Brigade Commander on 17 May. 'Fire shots at some useful target or get the hell out of it.'

The same day he was complaining bitterly to Austin Stack about Sinn Féin politicians making things 'intolerable' for militants like himself. 'The policy now seems to be to squeeze out anyone who is tainted with strong fighting ideas, or should I say the utility of fighting.' He was particularly critical of the party's Executive Committee, which he described as 'a Standing Committee of malcontents' who were 'inclined to be even less militant and more political and theoretical.' In short, they were talkers and thinkers, rather than men of action, and he was a man of action. 'We have too many of the bargaining type already,' Collins grumbled. 'I am not sure that our movement or part of it at any rate is alive to the developing situation.'

Describing himself as 'only an onlooker' at the Executive Committee meetings, he complained that the moderates were in control.

When Harry Boland went to the United States to make preparations for de Valera's forthcoming tour, the party replaced him as National Secretary with Hannah Sheehy-Skeffington the wife of a pacifist murdered during the Easter Rising. Collins was appalled. Not only had Boland been replaced by a moderate, but the party went on to announce that he was replaced because he was out of the country. With this announcement, Collins fumed, 'our people give away in a moment what the Detective Division has been unable to find out in five weeks.'

He clearly felt a lot of hostility towards himself and his militant views. There were 'rumours, whispering, suggestions of differences between certain people,' all of which he described as rather pitiful and disheartening. It belied the national unity of which de Valera boasted and it tended towards confusion about the best way of achieving the national aims. 'At the moment I'm awfully fed up,' Collins exclaimed.

'Things are not going very smoothly', he was still writing three weeks later. 'All sorts of miserable little under-currents are working and the effect is anything but good.'

6. 'We Struck at Individuals'

In early 1919 Collins was formally appointed Director of Intelligence of the Irish Volunteers. It was in this area that he made his greatest mark.

For centuries the British were renowned for their secret services. In the Great War just ended, British Intelligence had functioned magnificently, breaking German codes and using the information to steer the United States into the war against Germany. During the Second World War, Britain would again break the German codes, but in between those two wars British Intelligence suffered at the hands of Collins, who made their people look like bungling amateurs, for a time at any rate.

As Director of Organisation Collins had put together an escape network that was later emulated by Britain's MI9 in the Second World War. Eamonn Duggan had been appointed as the first Director of Intelligence for the Volunteers, but never built up much of an organisation. It was merely an adjunct of his legal practice, and he had only one man working for him.

Collins, on the other hand, set up a far-reaching network, incorporating intelligence gathering, counter-intelligence, and matters relating to prison escapes and smuggling, both arms and people. He was the brains behind the whole network and his industry was phenomenal. He retained personal control over work similar to that done by three different intelligence agencies in Britain, MI5, MI6, and MI9.

An intelligence office was set up at 3 Crow Street over the print shop of J. F. Fowler, with Liam Tobin in charge. A tall, gaunt man with a cynical expression, he was a fairly inconspicuous individual. Unlike Collins, who bounded from place to place, Tobin moved listlessly, walking with his arms hanging straight by his sides, but his appearance was deceptive. He ran the Intelligence office at 3 Crow Street, which Collins never even visited. Tom Cullen and Frank Thornton were Tobin's principal lieutenants. A staff was built up with people like Frank Saurin, Joe Guilfoyle, Charlie Dalton, and Joe Dolan. With their help Collins set about demoralising the police.

There were two separate police forces in Ireland at the time, the Royal Irish Constabulary (RIC) and the Dublin Metropolitan Police (DMP). The latter which functioned only in the Dublin area, was divided into seven divisions, lettered A through G. Divisions A, B, C and D were uniformed police dealing with different sections of the city, while E and F dealt with the outskirts, and G was an overall division of plain clothes detectives dealing with all types of crime, not just political crimes.

The intelligence staff were Collins' aides. Their initial task was to gather as much information as possible about the police, especially G Division. Information such as where they lived, and the names of members of their families would prove invaluable to Collins in the coming months. His agents were a whole range of people, with no one too humble to be of use. Maids in guest houses and hotels, porters, bar-tenders, sailors, railwaymen, postmen, sorters, telephone and telegraph operators, warders, and ordinary policemen all played an important part, and he had the splendid ability of making each feel important, even though he rarely, if ever, thanked them for what they were doing.

'Why should I thank people for doing their part?' he would ask. 'Isn't Ireland their country as well as mine?'

When Collins gave Tom Gay £5 for Detective Sergeant Kavanagh after the latter supplied the names of those about to be arrested in connection with the so-called German Plot, there was something contemptuous about the gesture. Gay recognised this and returned the money to Collins a few days later.

'Didn't you give him the money!' Collins exclaimed.

'No.'

'You didn't think he'd take it?'

'No.'

'A bloody queer G man!'

It was, of course, early days yet and Collins was still very raw. In his contempt for the police force, it did not seem to occur to him that there could be patriotic Irishmen in the police as in any other walk of life. But, unlike others in the movement, he soon learned this lesson and turned it to the advantage of the cause.

At the heart of his intelligence gathering network were his police spies. The first to be recruited were the two G men, Joe Kavanagh and Ned Broy, who had warned about impending arrests at the time of the so-called German Plot. Kavanagh – a short, dapper, sixty year old Dubliner, with a waxed moustache – had taken part in identifying leaders of the Easter Rising at

Richmond Barracks, and had obviously come to regret his role. He was now secretly committed to Sinn Féin, though he didn't have long to live. He died of a heart attack in 1920, by which time he had been of invaluable service to Collins.

Broy, on the other hand, was only in his mid-twenties. A rather stooped individual with a broad face, he was a native of County Kildare and worked as an official typist at G Division's headquarters in Great Brunswick (now Pearse) Street. He thought of himself strictly as an Irishman and had been looking for somebody within Sinn Féin who could make proper use of important information which he was prepared to pass on. Then one day in January 1919 he was asked to see Collins.

'Immediately I met him,' Broy later explained, 'I knew he was the man who could beat the British and I decided to work for him from then on.'

As a confidential typist Broy was in a particularly sensitive position. When he typed any report of interest to Collins, he simply inserted an extra carbon and made an additional copy. He then passed these on at weekly meetings which he and Kavanagh had with Collins at the home of the latter's librarian friend, Thomas Gay.

'If we were to stand up against the powerful military organisation arrayed against us,' Collins later explained, 'something more was necessary than a guerrilla war in which small bands of our warriors, aided by their knowledge of the country, attacked the larger forces of the enemy and reduced their numbers. England could always reinforce her army. . . She could replace every soldier that she lost.'

'But,' he added, 'there were others indispensable for her purposes which [sic] were not so easily replaced. To paralyse the British machine it was necessary to strike at individuals. Without her spies England was helpless. It was only by means of their accumulated and accumulating knowledge that the British machine could operate.'

Collins basically considered the DMP and RIC as spies. Detectives from G Division had, after all, segregated the leaders from the rank and file at Richmond Barracks after the Easter Rising. And the British had relied on the RIC to select those who were deported from other parts of the country in the aftermath of the rebellion. 'Without their police throughout the country, how could they find the men they "wanted"?' he asked.

Without the help of such people the British administration

would be virtually blind, so Collins decided to eliminate them. They would be warned to desist from political work, and if they did not heed the warning, they would be shot.

'Spies are not so ready to step into the shoes of their departed confederates as are soldiers to fill up the front line in honourable battle,' he noted. 'And even when the new spy stepped into the shoes of the old one, he could not step into the old one's knowledge. . . We struck at individuals and by so doing we cut their lines of communication and we shook their morale,' he explained afterwards. But, of course, he first had to learn who were the most effective detectives.

His audacity seemed to know no bounds. Around midnight on the night of 7 April 1919, he actually entered the G Division headquarters and had Broy lock him into the documents room, where he spent several hours going through the files, including his own. He later bragged, with characteristic vanity, that his file mentioned he came from 'a brainy Cork family.' These files gave him an invaluable perspective on what the G Division knew, and its most active detectives. As far as he was concerned they were the eyes of Dublin Castle and he was determined that if they were not going to close their eyes, he would shut them.

The detectives were given a very public warning two nights later. Volunteers raided the home of Detective Sergeant Halley, and they held up Detective Constable O'Brien in the street, and bound and gagged him. Neither man was hurt, but it was a warning to their colleagues that the Volunteers could and would strike at them in the streets or in their homes.

While Collins planned to kill detectives who did not heed the warning, de Valera favoured what was called the moral resistance approach. He merely proposed that the police should 'be ostracised socially by the people of Ireland'. The Dáil formally approved of this approach, and de Valera sought to keep militants like Collins in check by giving the Standing Committee of Sinn Féin a strong voice in policy matters.

In the face of the organised ostracisation many policemen resigned. Others continued, of course. Most had spent their whole working lives in the police force, and many were too old to find other employment. Some were not afraid of Sinn Féin.

Detective Sergeant Patrick Smith, known to the Volunteers as 'Dog Smith', had arrested Piaras Beaslaí for making a seditious speech and found some incriminating documents on him. Collins and Harry Boland tried to induce Smith not to produce those documents in court but the detective ignored them, with the result that Beaslaí was sentenced to two years in jail, instead of the two months he might otherwise have expected. It was obvious that mere ostracisation was not going to intimidate Smith.

Collins was therefore authorised by Richard Mulcahy as Chief-of-Staff and Cathal Brugha as Minister for Defence to eliminate Smith, and to establish a full-time service unit to undertake the assassination of detectives who persisted in political work against the movement, as well as any spies who helped them. The Squad, as it was known, was basically the counter-intelligence arm of Collins' network. It began with about seven men and was soon extended to twelve, who were sometimes irreverently known as 'The Twelve Apostles', and the name stuck even after more were included.

Mick MacDonald, a colleague from Frongoch days, was the first head of the Squad, which included his brother-in-law Tom Keogh, and other inmates from Frongoch, like Bill Stapleton and Jim Slattery. They were never intended as a bodyguard for Collins, as has been suggested. Instead they were a full-time assassination team, made up of clerks, tradesmen, and general workers, who were paid £4.10 a week.

Initially the Squad's meeting place was in Oriel House, but it soon moved to a builders' yard near Dublin Castle. There was a sign over the main gate, 'Geo. Moreland Cabinet Maker.' Vinny Byrne was a master carpenter and did carpentry work in the yard while not engaged in Squad business, but most prospective customers who ventured into the yard were discouraged by outrageously long delivery dates.

'Our chief function,' Bill Stapleton recalled, 'was the extermination of British spies and individuals.' Their first job was to eliminate Smith, who was shot and mortally wounded outside his Drumcondra home on the night of 30 July 1919. '"Dog" Smith had been warned on a number of occasions to lay off Republicans or he would be shot,' one of those who took part in the assassination later explained. 'He persisted and met the fate he asked for.'

As Smith lay dying Dublin Castle's reaction was to ban Sinn Féin, an ill-conceived act that played directly into the hands of Collins, who would henceforth have little diffi-culty in out-manoeuvring Sinn Féin moderates and imple-menting a more militant policy. The checks that de Valera had placed on the militants were wiped out by the banning of the political wing of the movement, which prompted one leading British civil servant to conclude that the Castle regime was 'almost woodenly stupid and quite devoid of imagination'.

'In Ireland the Sinn Féin party – representing the great majority of Irishmen – had been proclaimed as an illegal organisation!' Sir Warren Fisher wrote in near disbelief after he had been sent to investigate the Irish situation a few months later. 'Imagine the result on public opinion in Great Britain of a similar act by the Executive towards a political party (or the women's suffrage movement)!'

During August Collins launched the National Loan to raise a quarter of a million pounds throughout Ireland within twelve months. As expected the British proscribed the loan, and he became all the more determined to ensure its success.

The authorities arrested anyone selling bonds and even people speaking in favour of the scheme. By mid-September Collins was writing about 'the usual daily round' of raids and counter-raids. 'Repression becomes more and more marked,' he wrote. 'On our side the spirit is if anything improving to meet the ever increasing demands which the enemy make.'

On 12 September the British proscribed Dáil Éireann and thus compounded the mistake in banning Sinn Féin. What little ground that had been left was cut from under the moderates. In the next nine months the Dáil met only once. The militants took firm control, and the IVF changed its name to Irish Republican Army (IRA), dedicated to driving the British out of Ireland. Soon Collins would have that state of general disorder which he had called for back in March.

On the day the Dáil was proscribed, the DMP raided Sinn Féin headquarters at 6 Harcourt Street. Collins was in his finance office upstairs as the raiding party burst into the building. 'It was only by almost a miracle I was not landed,' he wrote next day. 'It so happened the particular detective who came into the room where I was did not know me, which gave me an opportunity of eluding him.'

The detective asked Collins about some documents he was carrying.

'What have they got to do with you?' Collins snapped in reply. 'A nice job you've got, spying on your countrymen.'

The detective was apparently so taken aback by the confident show of insolence that he made no effort to prevent Collins going upstairs to the caretaker's living quarters on the top floor. There, Collins climbed out the skylight and hid on the roof of the nearby Ivanhoe Hotel. Two prominent members of the party were arrested in the building, Ernest Blythe, and Pádraig O'Keeffe, an acting National Secretary.

One of the police involved in the raid was Detective Constable Daniel Hoey, a particular thorn in the side of the Volunteers going back to before 1916. Realising that Collins had escaped, O'Keeffe knew the detective was in trouble.

'You're for it tonight, Hoey,' he warned.

O'Keeffe might well have been sentenced to more than a couple of months in jail, if Hoey had been able to testify about the threat, but the warning was prophetic. Hoey was shot and killed by the Squad that night in Townsend Street just around the corner from G Division's headquarters.

Collins opened new offices at 76 Harcourt Street, and this time certain precautions were taken to ensure an escape route for himself and a hiding place for important papers. Batt O'Connor built a small secret closet into a wall to store documents, and a bell was rigged up outside Collins' office on the top floor so that the caretaker downstairs could warn him if the building was being raided. There was a ladder to a skylight and arrangements were made with the porter of the Standard Hotel, two doors away, to leave the hotel skylight unlocked at all times.

The more the Crown authorities tried to interfere with Collins' efforts to promote the National Loan, the more determined he became to ensure its success, despite mounting promotional problems. 'We are having extreme difficulties in advertising as far as newspapers are concerned,' he noted. It was illegal for the press to carry advertisements for the loan, and the *Cork Examiner* and some twenty-one local newspapers were suppressed between 17 September and 7 October for carrying such advertisements.

'The enemy's chief offensive here at the moment is directed against the loan,' Collins wrote to de Valera on 14 October. 'Men are being arrested for making public reference to the subject.'

A novel way of promoting the campaign was found – by using a short movie clip, showing Collins and Diamuid O'Hegarty sitting at a table outside Pearse's old school, signing bonds being purchased by Pearse's mother, Clarke's widow, and Connolly's daughter. Armed Volunteers raided cinemas and ordered projectionists to run the brief clip; they would then hightail it with the film before the police or military could be called. Hitherto the name of Michael Collins was largely unknown outside separatist circles, but the film would project his name before the public as never before and, as the Crown forces concentrated on suppressing the loan, his reputation grew to the point where he became the most wanted man in the country.

'That film of yourself and Hegarty selling Bonds brought tears to me eyes,' Harry Boland wrote from the United States. 'Gee Boy! You are some movie actor. Nobody could resist buying a Bond and we having such a handsome Minister for Finance.'

While deeply involved in fund-raising, Collins also became involved with Dan Breen in a plot to assassinate the Lord Lieutenant, Lord French. Breen and three colleagues, who had killed the two RIC men escorting the explosive consignment at Soloheadbeg in January, had come to Dublin looking for more meaningful action.

Their 'only regret' about Soloheadbeg was that they had only killed two policemen, and not more. 'Six would have created a better impression than a mere two,' Breen wrote. 'We felt bigger game was needed,' he added.

Collins shared their impatience, but he had no intention of getting involved in a numbers game. He believed in striking at individuals who were providing useful service to the British. The person with the highest profile in this regard was Lord French, a symbol of Britain's domination as well as Lloyd George's most influential adviser on Irish matters at the time. Brugha and Mulcahy agreed, so Collins ordered members of the Squad to join with four Tipperarymen in a plan to assassinate the viceroy.

'For three long months we watched, planned and waited,' according to Breen. 'Mick Collins was with us on the first occasion that we lay in ambush.' He had learned that French was returning from England through Dun Laoghaire that night and the ambush was set up at the junction of Suffolk and Trinity Streets. They waited until dawn but the viceroy never showed. Nothing happened either on a number of other occasions because French – mindful of the need for extreme caution – repeatedly altered his route at the last moment. Of course, Collins was much too busy to be personally involved in all of the attempts. He was busy on other matters, like building up his Intelligence network, or springing Stack from jail.

He was already taking a particularly active interest in supervising arrangements for the escape of Stack. For more than a year he had been planning to spring him, first from Dundalk Jail and then Belfast Jail, but on each occasion Stack was moved before arrangements could be finalised. Now he was in Strangeways Jail in Manchester.

Collins actually visited Stack in the prison to discuss plans for the escape which was finally set for 25 October. Some twenty men were posted outside the jail, under Rory O'Connor. Basically the same technique was used as in the mass escape from Mountjoy. Piaras Beaslaí had been involved in the escape, but had been recaptured by the ill-fated 'Dog' Smith, and he was again involved in this break in which Stack, himself, and four others managed to escape. They were taken to safe houses in the Manchester and Liverpool area while Collins personally crossed the Irish Sea to make arrangements for their return to Dublin.

The more Collins' notoriety grew, the more willing some people were to work for him, and the fact that he was President of the Supreme Council of the IRB probably helped in recruiting spies. A person in his position in a secret society was someone they could trust.

Kavanagh and Broy introduced a new detective, James McNamara, who was administrative assistant to the Assistant Police Commissioner in Dublin Castle. The son of a policeman, McNamara was a charming individual, and he joined Kavanagh and Broy in their weekly meetings with Collins in Tom Gay's home.

In September Collins learned that a Sergeant Jerry Maher of the RIC in Naas might be sympathetic. When an emissary approached Maher to work for Collins his eyes immediately lit up. 'You're the man I've been waiting for,' Maher replied.

He was working as a clerk for the District Inspector of the RIC, and he was able to feed Collins with information about various circulars from headquarters, as well as current codes being used. At times in the coming months Collins would have dispatches decoded and circulated to Brigade Intelligence Officers before some of the RIC inspectors had decoded their own messages.

Collins also had at least two other sources for the police codes. Maurice MacCarthy, an RIC sergeant stationed in Belfast was one, and the other was a cousin of his own working for Dublin Castle. The cousin, Nancy O'Brien, had spent some years working in the post office in London and was brought to Dublin as a cipher clerk to decode messages. She was selected, she was told, because the Castle authorities wanted someone they could trust, because Collins was getting some messages even before the British officers for whom they were intended. She, of course, promptly went to Collins.

'Well, Christ! I don't know how they've held their Empire for so long,' Collins exclaimed. 'What a bloody intelligence service they have.'

Sergeant T. J. McElligott had been dismissed from the RIC because of his Sinn Féin sympathies, and he secretly went to work for Collins as a kind of police union organiser. Ostensibly he was trying to improve the pay and conditions of the RIC, but, in fact, he was engaged in black propaganda trying to undermine the morale of the force by sowing seeds of discord.

When the police went on strike in London. Collins sent McElligott there to make some useful contacts. At strike head-quarters he met a man using the name of Jameson, who was posing as a Marxist sympathiser but was actually a Secret Service agent. Shortly afterwards he turned up in Dublin and very nearly entrapped Collins, but this is getting ahead of the story.

On 8 November Collins was in his new financial office in 76 Harcourt Street when it was raided. The staff managed to get the important papers into the secret closet, while he headed for the skylight with an attache case. The Standard Hotel's skylight was unlocked as arranged but, to his horror, he found that it was directly above a stairwell, which meant that he had to make a dangerous jump across the landing. 'Just as I got through the hotel skylight I saw a khaki helmet appear out of the skylight of No. 76,' he told colleagues that evening. 'I flung my bag across, commended myself to Providence, and jumped.' Although he hurt himself in the process, he was in great spirits that evening as he recounted what happened.

Three members of the Dáil were arrested in the raid, along with three members of the Volunteer headquarters staff, but the police failed to find the secret closet. One of the uniformed policemen ordered to search the building was Constable David Nelligan, who had no intention of trying to find anything. 'I went upstairs and counted the roses on the wallpaper until the raid was over,' he later wrote.

'They got no document of importance, so that the only

disorganisation is through the seizure of the staff,' Collins wrote. 'The enemy is certainly very keen at the moment in preventing the Dáil loan being a success, so that it becomes a more pressing duty than ever that every supporter of the Republic should increase his efforts.'

The latest raid on his office was probably in response to an attack, the previous day, on Detective Sergeant Wharton. He was shot and seriously wounded by a member of the Squad as he walked by St Stephen's Green. A native of Killarney, the detective remained active in political work despite repeated warnings. An innocent news vendor at the scene was later arrested and convicted of being involved in the attack. Although Wharton survived, his injuries forced him to resign from the police force, but he was luckier than his fellow Kerryman, Detective Sergeant Johnny Barton who arrested the news vendor. He was shot near the G Division headquarters at the height of the evening rush hour on 30 November.

'What did I do?' he moaned repeatedly as he lay dying. He had been in G Division only two months. In Collins' eyes, however, he had committed the unforgivable sin of trying to find Wharton's assailants.

While it was believed that Collins moved about in disguise, highly armed and well-protected, he usually went alone, unarmed, on a bicycle, without any disguise. Some of the detectives knew him, but he had so terrorised the G Division that they were afraid to apprehend him, lest the faceless people supposedly protecting him would come to his rescue, or take revenge on the detective or his family at some later date. Of course, attacking members of anyone's family would have been totally out of character for Collins, but his enemies were not to know this. They knew only of his ruthless reputation, and he exploited it to the full.

One can imagine the scene as Collins recognised a detective on a tram. He would sit down next to him, ask about specific members of the detective's family, or colleagues in the DMP, and – before alighting – assure the detective it would be safe for him to get off the tram, *at some later stop*.

One day in the street Batt O'Connor became uneasy at the way two DMP looked at Collins. They seemed to recognise him, but he was unperturbed.

'Even if they recognised me,' Collins said, 'they would be afraid to report they saw me.'

Anyway, if they did report, it would take the DMP an hour to muster the necessary force to seize him. 'And, of course,' he added, 'all the time I would wait here until they were ready to come along!'

He never stayed in any one place very long; he had difficulty in sitting still. He had something to do, somebody to see, or somewhere to go. Collins was always on the go, though he never thought of himself as being 'on the run'. Wanted men frequently developed a habit of venturing forth only with care. Before leaving a building they would sneak a furtive glance to make sure there were no police around, whereas Collins had contempt for such practices. He just bounded out a door in a carefree, self-confident manner without betraying the slightest indication he was trying to evade anybody. 'I do not allow myself to feel I am on the run,' he explained. 'That is my safeguard. It prevents me from acting in a manner likely to arouse suspicion.'.

When the police started looking for him in May, he moved from the Munster Hotel, but in the autumn he felt safe enough to move back again. By acting as he did he gave the distinct impression of not being afraid of the detectives; they were left to ponder whether he was crazy or just very well protected. In either case he was not someone to mess with.

7. 'Spies Beware'

Faced with the demise of the DMP's most active detectives, Lord French set up a three man committee to consider what to do about the deteriorating intelligence situation from the British point of view. The three were the acting Inspector General of the RIC, the Assistant Under Secretary at Dublin Castle, and a Resident Magistrate named Alan Bell. The latter, a former RIC man, was particularly close to French and had a great deal of investigative experience going back to the troubles of the 1880s.

The committee reported on 7 December that 'an organised conspiracy of murder, outrage and intimidation has existed for sometime past' with the aim of undermining the police forces. Even though the first police had been killed in Tipperary, the committee concluded that 'Dublin City is the storm centre and mainspring of it all.' To remedy the situation it was proposed that the Sinn Féin movement should be infiltrated with spies and some selected leaders should be assassinated. 'We are inclined to think that the shooting of a few would-be assassins would have an excellent effect,' the committee reported. 'Up to the present they have escaped with impunity. We think that this should be tried as soon as possible.'

This was really a very important day in the life of Collins. He returned to where he was staying at the Munster Hotel to find a police raid in progress. The DMP were looking for him, but he mingled outside with spectators in the street. He knew that Detective Inspector Bruton was aware he lived there, and he apparently blamed him for the raid. The Squad were ordered to kill Bruton, though this was easier ordered than done. Bruton ventured out of Dublin Castle only under armed escort, and he took the precaution of not developing any routine. Soon the attempt to kill him began to take on the aspects of a farce as Squad members lurked near a Castle entrance.

'Misters! They're not here today,' a newsboy shouted one day.

That was enough. If the boy could twig them, it was time to move to other matters. In any event the finger of suspicion was soon transferred from Bruton to a spy who had infiltrated Collins' network. H.H. Quinlisk from Wexford had been one of the prisoners-of-war recruited by Casement for his Irish Brigade in Germany. With credentials like that Quinlisk was easily accepted in Sinn Féin quarters, especially after Robert Brennan, introduced him to Seán Ó Muirthile, the Secretary of the Supreme Council of the IRB. Quinlisk, or Quinn as he called himself, cut a dashing figure and was quite a man for the ladies. 'He was always immaculately dressed and one would have said that with his good looks, his self-assurance and general *bon-homie*, he would have got anywhere,' according to Brennan. 'He liked to give the impression that he was in on all of Mick Collins secrets.'

As a result of his enlistment in the Irish Brigade, he had been denied backpay for the period of his imprisonment in Germany. Collins helped him out financially, and Quinlisk stayed for a time at the Munster Hotel but he wanted more. On 11 November he wrote to the Under Secretary at Dublin Castle, mentioning his background and offering to furnish information. 'I was the man who assisted Casement in Germany and since coming home I have been connected with Sinn Féin,' he wrote. 'I have decided to tell all I know of that organisation and my information would be of use to the authorities. The scoundrel Michael Collins has treated me scurvily and I now am going to wash my hands of the whole business.'

He was brought to G Division headquarters to make a statement which Broy typed up and, of course, furnished a copy to Collins. But Quinlisk had taken the precaution of telling Collins that he had gone to DMP merely to get a passport so he could emigrate to the United States. He said the police put pressure on him to inform on Collins, offering money and promised to make arrangements for him to get his wartime backpay. He told Collins that he was merely pretending to go along with police.

Following the raid on the Munster Hotel, Collins found it necessary to move, though he did return there weekly. The owner, a Miss McCarthy, an aunt of Fionán Lynch, continued to do his laundry for him. For the next nineteen months he moved about, never staying in any one place for very long. 'Living in such turmoil,' he wrote to Hannie, 'it's not all that easy to be clear on all matters at all times.' Yet he maintained a very regular daily routine.

After his office at 76 Harcourt Street was raided in November, he opened a new finance officer at 22 Mary Street. Like his other offices, it was on a busy thoroughfare with a lot of passing traffic, so that the comings and goings of strangers would not attract attention, as they would if the offices had been placed in some quiet, out-of-the-way location. The Mary Street office survived for about eighteen months. He also had another finance office at 29 Mary Street and he set up a new Intelligence office at 5 Mespil Road. He kept papers in the home of Eileen McGrane at 21 Dawson Street, and had gold hidden in a house owned by Batt O'Connor at 3 St Andrew's Terrace, and also in O'Connor's home at 1 Brendan's Road, Donnybrook.

In the morning he would go to his intelligence office in Mespil Road. This was only known to his secretary Susan Mason, Tobin, O'Reilly, and a couple of other people. He did not meet people there. Afterwards he would cycle over to his finance office in Mary Street, and he would have lunch at either Batt O'Connor's home in Donnybrook or in Pádraig O'Keeffe's wife's restaurant in Camden Street. He would meet people in either of these two places or in one of the many 'joints' that he used about the city.

There was a whole cluster of these in the north side of the city around the Rutland (now Parnell) Square area. 'Joint No. 1' was Vaughan's Hotel at 29 Rutland Square. It was a kind of clearing-house for him. People visiting from outside Dublin wishing to meet him for the first time would go to Vaughan's, where the porter, Christy Harte, was usually able to pass on a message to him. 'Joint No. 2' was Liam Devlin's pub at 69 Parnell Street on the south side of the square. Here Collins met a more selected group of people, like members of the Dublin Brigade, and he met warders from Mountjoy Jail in Jim Kirwin's Bar on the same street. Other 'joints' around the square included No. 4, the old headquarters of the Irish Volunteers; No. 20, Bamba Hall; No. 41, Irish National Forresters Hall; No. 46 the Keating Branch of the Gaelic League. Nearby were other joints, Barry's Hotel on Great Denmark Street and Fleming's Hotel in Gardiner Row. He met railwaymen carrying despatches to and from Belfast at Phil Sheerin's Coolevin Dairies in Amiens Street, police contacts in the Bannon brother's pub in Upper Abbey Street, and sailors with news from Britain in Foley Street at Pat Shanahan's bar, which was also the haunt of the Dan Breen and the Soloheadbeg gang.

They and the Squad finally caught up with Lord French on 19 December. He had gone to his country residence in Roscommon, and Collins sent a man there to report when the Lord

Lieutenant left for Dublin. An ambush was then prepared at Ashtown Cross, not far from the Vice Regal Lodge in the Phoenix Park, Dublin. The attempt was bungled, however, and the only fatality was one of the ambushers who was apparently caught in cross-fire.

After his escape French was highly critical of G Division. 'Our Secret Service is simply non-existent,' he complained. 'What masquerades for such a service is nothing but a delusion and a snare. The DMP are absolutely demoralised and the RIC will be in the same case very soon if we do not quickly set our house in order.'

Detective Inspector W. C. Forbes Redmond was brought from Belfast as Assistant Commissioner to re-organise G Division, and he brought a number of his own people to work under cover. Not knowing Dublin, he had to have someone as a guide to the city, so he naturally used his administrative assistant, Jim McNamara. Redmond set about to capture Collins, and he came quite close with the help of a Secret Service agent who wormed his way into Collins' confidence.

The agent was John Charles Byrne, alias Jameson, the supposed Marxist whom T. J. McElligott had met at the police strike headquarters in London. He had come to Dublin with a letter of introduction from Art O'Brien, the Sinn Féin representative in Britain. Posing as a revolutionary anxious to undermine the British system, Byrne offered to supply weapons, and arrangements were made for him to meet Collins, Mulcahy and Rory O'Connor at the Home Farm Produce Shop in Camden Street. They met again the following day at the Ranelagh home of Mrs Wyse Power, a member of the Sinn Féin Executive.

'What he was delaying about that prevented him getting us caught with him, at least on the second of these occasions, I don't know,' Mulcahy remarked. Byrne did make arrangements to have Collins arrested after a third meeting at the home of Batt O'Connor on 16 January 1920.

Redmond had one of his own undercover men watching the house, but that man did not know Collins and by a stroke of good luck Liam Tobin, who also happened to be at the house, left with Byrne and the lookout – assuming that Tobin was Collins – intercepted Redmond on Morehampton Road as he approached with a lorry load of troops to raid O'Connor's house. The raid was promptly called, off but Redmond had brought McNamara with him, and also used him as a guide that night when he decided to keep O'Connor's house under personal observation.

By next day Collins had been briefed. He was due to have dinner again at O'Connor's house, but he gave it a skip. When Redmond and the police arrived, there was no one in the house, other than O'Connor's wife and children. He left promising not to bother her again, a prophetic promise as it turned out.

Redmond had already made a fatal mistake when a detective had come to him with a grievance over some of his changes in G Division, and he dismissed the complaint with some disparaging comments about G Division as a whole. 'You are a bright lot!' Redmond reportedly said. 'Not one of you has been able to get on to Collins' track for a month, and here is a man only two days in Dublin and has already seen him.'

The disgruntled detective duly mentioned this to Broy, who promptly informed Collins. Together with the information from McNamara, the spotlight of suspicion was immediately cast on Byrne. He had not only just arrived from London but had also had a meeting with Collins.

Tobin had distrusted Byrne from the outset, but had problems convincing Collins, who liked the unusual visitor. The thirty-four year old Byrne was clearly an adventurer. Small with a very muscular build, he had a whole series of tattoos on his arms and hands. There were Japanese women, snakes, flowers and a bird. He had a snake ring tattooed on the third finger of his right hand and two rings tattooed on his left hand. He also had a strange fascination for birds, the feathered variety; he kept a number in cages in his hotel room.

Collins and Tobin decided to bait a trap for Byrne, by giving him information to believe that important documents were being stored in the home of a former Lord Mayor of Dublin, J.J. Farrell of 9 Iona Road. The Castle authorities had no grounds for suspecting him, because he had no sympathy whatever for Sinn Féin. The greatest moment of his life had been when he received the King. Collins' men kept an eye on Farrell's house, and had a great laugh when the police raided it and forced the former mayor to stand outside in his night attire. 'You are raiding your friends,' Farrell protested. 'Do you know I received the King? I had twenty minutes conversation with him.'

Of course the raid looked particularly bad for Jameson, and he promptly left the country. On the night of 20 January 1920 Collins was tipped off that Redmond planned a raid that night on Cullenswood House, where Collins had a basement office and

Mulcahy had a top-floor flat with his wife. Cullen and Thornton roused Mulcahy from his bed, and he spent the remainder of the night with a friend a short distance away. Redmond was becoming a real thorn, and Collins gave the Squad orders to eliminate him.

'If we don't get that man, he'll get us and soon,' Collins warned the Squad.

Redmond really made a soft target, because he under-estimated his opponents. Nattily dressed in civilian clothes, topped off by a bowler hat, he looked more like a stockbroker than a policeman. He stayed at the Standard Hotel in Harcourt Street and walked to work at Dublin Castle and back without an escort, though he did take the precaution of wearing a bullet-proof vest.

That evening the Squad got their chance as Redmond returned to his hotel. 'We knew he had a bullet-proof waistcoat,' Joe Dolan of the Squad later explained with childish giggle. 'So we shot him in the head.'

Following Redmond's death, his own undercover detectives pulled out and returned to Belfast, and thereafter G Division 'ceased to affect the situation,' according to British Military intelligence.

Stunned by Redmond's killing, Dublin Castle offered £10,000 rewards for information leading to the arrest and conviction of the person responsible for his death. This was probably where the story about the big reward for Collins' arrest originated. He was the one who had given the order to kill Redmond. Rewards of £5,000 had already been offered in connection with the deaths of the three other DMP detectives, Smith, Hoey, and Barton, and these rewards were now doubled. As Collins had ordered all four killings, there was a handsome accumulative reward for the evidence to convict him, though the authorities never officially offered a reward for his actual capture.

The British gradually began to fight back. On 24 February a curfew was introduced from midnight until five o'clock in the morning. 'Last night,' Collins wrote next day, 'the city of Dublin was like a city of the dead. It is the English way of restoring peace to this country.' In the following weeks he would complain of growing repression. 'By night the streets of Dublin are like streets of a beleaguered city – none abroad save the military forces of the enemy fully equipped for all the purposes and usages of war.'

The British were infiltrating a whole series of undercover people into Ireland, and their established agents made desperate efforts to entrap Collins. Quinlisk, who had lost touch with him following the raid on the Munster Hotel, began making desperate efforts to contact him. By now, however, Collins had firm evidence of his treachery – having got his hands on Quinlisk's actual letter offering his services to Dublin Castle. But Collins did not ask the Squad to try to take out the spy immediately. Instead he tried to use him as bait to get at Detective Superintendent Brien of the DMP. The Squad had been trying to kill him for some time, but Brien rarely moved outside the walls of Dublin Castle.

Seán Ó Muirthile was assigned to keep Quinlisk busy, while one of the Squad telephoned the Castle to say that Quinlisk had vital information and would meet Brien outside the offices of the *Evening Mail*, just outside the Castle, at a certain time.

Brien turned up but something spooked him before the Squad could get a shot at him. He darted back into the cover of Dublin Castle.

Collins learned afterwards that the Detective Superintendent had twigged he was being set up and blamed Quinlisk, who explained that he had been detained all night by Ó Muirthile.

'You're in the soup,' Collins told Ó Muirthile with a laugh.

Quinlisk should have had the good sense to quit at that point, but he persisted in his efforts to see Collins. So a trap was set. He was told that Collins was out of town and would meet him that night at Wren's Hotel in Cork City.

Liam Archer, one of Collins' telegraphist agents at the GPO duly intercepted a coded message to the District Inspector of the RIC at Union Quay, Cork. 'Tonight at midnight surround Wren's Hotel, Winthrop Street,Cork,' the message read when decoded. 'Collins and others will be there. Expect shooting as he is a dangerous man and heavily armed.'

'*tAnam an Diabhal*,' Collins exclaimed with a laugh on reading the message. 'They'll play *sighle caoch* with the place.'

RIC duly raided the hotel and, of course, found nothing. Quinlisk stayed in Cork searching for Collins. On the night of 18 February he was met by some members of the IRA, who – promising to take him to Collins – took him outside the city and shot him dead and pinned a note to his body – 'Spies Beware.'

District Inspector MacDonagh of the RIC had made the mistake of looking for Collins in Cork, and he was gunned down on the street in the city three weeks later. No evidence was ever produced to suggest Collins had called for the attempt on his life. But even if the IRA in Cork had done so without directions from Dublin, the ultimate message to the police was still the same – looking for Collins was dangerous to their health.

Around this time Byrne, alias Jameson, returned with a suitcase of revolvers. Tobin took the guns and pretended to leave them in a business premises on Bachelor's Walk, which he said was an arms' dump for the IRA. When the premises were raided that night, Collins was finally convinced of Byrne's duplicity. Members of the Squad called for Byrne at the Grenville Hotel on Sackville Street on the afternoon of 2 March on the pretext of taking him to Collins' hide-out, but they brought him to the grounds of a lunatic asylum in Glasnevin instead.

Realising what was about to happen, he tried to bluff them about his friendship with Collins and Tobin, but the Squad members knew better. They asked him if he wished to pray.

'No,' he replied.

'We are only doing our duty,' one said to him.

'And I have done mine,' he replied, drawing himself to attention as they shot him twice, once in the head and the other through the heart. Some weeks later members of the British cabinet were told that Byrne had been 'the best Secret Service man we had'.

After Byrne another British agent also managed to meet Collins at O'Connor's home. Fergus Bryan Molloy was also offering to procure arms. He was a soldier working for the Secret Service, but his fate was sealed when Collins' people in Dublin Castle warned him of Molloy's true purpose. He was gunned down by the Squad in broad daylight on South William Street three weeks to the day after Byrne.

On the day Byrne's body was returned to England, Alan Bell, the Resident Magistrate who had served on the secret committee which had called for 'the shooting of a few would-be assassins,' opened a much publicised inquiry into Sinn Féin funds. He was empowered to examine bank accounts in order to locate money deposited in the names of a number of party sympathisers.

Bell stayed out in Monkstown and travelled into the city each day on a tram. A police guard escorted him to and from the tram each day, but he travelled into the city alone. He was coming into the city as usual on the morning of 26 March when four men approached him as the tram reached Ballsbridge.

'Come on, Mr Bell, your time has come,' one of the men said.

Horrified passengers looked on as the Squad members dragged the elderly man into the street and shot him dead on the pavement. The killing of an old man like that provoked a storm of revulsion.

It was widely believed that he was killed because he was trying to find the National Loan money, though there were also published rumours that he had been investigating the attempt on the life of his friend, Lord French. One rather colourful story was published in the United States to the effect that Bell had 'arranged for a Scotland Yard detective to go to Mountjoy Prison, pose as a priest and "hear" confessions of political prisoners there.' The IRA supposedly learned of this and shot both Bell and the detective next day. The fact that no detective was killed next day, or indeed in the whole month of March, did not prevent the publication of the story.

Despite his frail elderly appearance, Bell had posed an extremely dangerous threat to Collins. He had, in fact, been directing Forbes Redmond, and he was also one of the architects of the policy which had led to the killing of Tomás MacCurtain, the Lord Mayor of Cork, three days earlier. This was not brought out at the time, presumably because Collins was not in a position to release the information without endangering his source in Dublin Castle.*

In any event, the bad publicity surrounding Bell's elimination, had some advantages, as far as Collins was concerned, because it acted as a very public warning to various individuals not to go looking for the loan money. Despite early misgivings he achieved the goal of raising a quarter of a million pounds. In fact the loan was over-subscribed by some forty per cent and more than £357,000 was collected. Of that the British only captured a mere £18,000.

*Reassessing the events more than a half a century later Tom Bower wrote that Collins had intercepted a letter from one British intelligence officer to another. The letter from Captain F. Harper Stove to Captain King (see page 94) was supposedly typed on the same Underwood typewriter as threatening letters to MacCurtain, and to both James McCarthy of Thurles and Tomas Dwyer of Barraduff, County Tipperary, who were killed under comparatively similar circumstances the following week. According to Bower the typewriter produced a curious alignment when a capital 'T' was followed by a lower case 'l', but he did not explain the even more curious sequence of those two letters. The use of the capital followed by a lower case letter would indicate the word or words had begun with the letter 't', but there is no word in the English language beginning with the letters 'tl'. In any event, Stove's letter to King was handwritten, not typed.

'From any point of view the seizure was insignificant,' Collins wrote, 'but you may rely upon it we shall see to the return of this money just as someday Ireland will exact her full reparation for all the stealings and seizures by the British in the past.'

8. 'We Got the Bugger'

Prior to 1920 the British cabinet was pre-occupied with other problems to devote much attention to Ireland, but the need to do something about the deteriorating situation gradually dawned on Lloyd George and his colleagues. They set about changing their own policy and undertook a thorough spring-cleaning of the Dublin Castle administration.

Sir Hamar Greenwood was appointed Chief Secretary, Sir John Anderson Under Secretary, and Andy Cope Assistant Under Secretary. General Sir Nevil Macready became Commander-in-Chief of British forces in Ireland, Major-General Henry Tudor took over at the head of the police, and Sir Ormonde Winter became chief of combined intelligence services.

From the outset Greenwood was determined to follow a hard-line policy. Even before visiting Ireland he 'talked the most awful tosh about shooting Sinn Féiners at sight, and without evidence, and frightfulness generally,' according to the Cabinet Secretary.

The British began to retaliate by using some of the IRA's tactics. In Cork during recent weeks, for instance, there had been the killings of Quinlisk and a number of constables, as well as the shooting of District Inspector MacDonagh. The police held Tomás MacCurtain responsible; he was both Lord Mayor of Cork and commander of the local IRA. Following the killing of another RIC constable on the night of 20 March a group of men with blackened faces forced their way into MacCurtain's home and shot him dead in front of his wife and daughter.

At the subsequent inquest there was evidence that the RIC had assisted the killers during the attack by cordoning off the area around the shop over which MacCurtain lived. The coroner's jury returned a verdict of murder against Lloyd George and various members of the British administration in Ireland, as well as District Inspector Swanzy of the RIC. He was one of a large number of Orangemen from Ulster stationed in Cork, and they were believed to have been implicated in the killing. Swanzy was transferred from Cork for his own protection.

Collins was deeply upset by the death of his friend, Mac-

Curtain; they had been quite close ever since their internment together in Frongoch. 'I have not very much heart in what I am doing today, thinking of poor Tomás,' Collins wrote to Terence MacSwiney, who was soon to take over from MacCurtain. 'It is surely the most appalling thing that has been done yet.'

Two similar killings took place on following nights in the Thurles area, where the RIC also contained a strong contingent of Orangemen. Collins complained that the British and 'their agents here, whether military, police or civil, are doing all they can to goad the people into premature action.' It had been with difficulty that Mulcahy and Collins had persuaded MacCurtain not to go ahead with plans to stage a 1916 style rebellion in Cork to commemorate the fourth anniversary of the Easter Rebellion. Terence MacSwiney, who succeeded MacCurtain as Lord Mayor, would not be easily goaded. He was quite prepared to suffer.

'This contest is one of endurance,' he declared in his inaugural address. 'It is not they who can inflict most, but they who can suffer most who will conquer.'

The other side's capacity for suffering was already showing signs of stress. Members of the RIC were not prepared to put up with the social ostracisation and attacks to which they were being subjected. Resignations from the force were running at more than two hundred a month in early 1920. It was not long before the British found it necessary to bring in new recruits from outside. The first of these arrived in Ireland on 25 March 1920. They had been recruited so hastily that there was not time to get them proper uniforms.

All wore the dark green caps and belts of the RIC, and some had the dark green tunics with military khaki pants, while others had khaki tunics and dark green pants. Most were veterans of the Great War who had been unable either to find civilian employment or to adjust to civilian life. The ten shillings a day, all found, was a relatively good wage for the time, especially for men who were desperate for a job. In view of the colour of their uniforms and the ruthless reputation they quickly acquired, they were called Black and Tans after a pack of hounds. The more active undoubtedly welcomed the name, because they – like Dan Breen – tended to see their enemy in terms of hunting 'game'.

Faced with the choice of British or Irish terrorists, the Irish people preferred their own; they hid them and supported them. As a result the Black and Tans quickly began to look on all civilians as their enemy and acted accordingly, thereby further alienating the Irish people from the Crown government.

The week after the arrival of the first contingent of Black and Tans, the IRA intensified its campaign. At Collins' suggestion tax offices throughout the country were fire bombed on the night of 3 April in an attempt to disrupt the British tax collecting apparatus. At the same time more than 350 unoccupied RIC barracks were burned to the ground.

When the British government discussed what to do about the Irish situation, General Macready advocated making the security forces mobile enough to surprise IRA bands, but Sir Henry Wilson, the Chief of Imperial General Staff, dismissed this idea as useless. He wanted instead, 'to collect the names of Sinn Féiners by districts; proclaim them on church doors all over the country; and whenever a policeman is murdered, pick 5 by lot and shoot them!' One could hardly imagine anything more likely to provoke the indignation of Irish people than to defile their churches in such a barbarous manner.

'Somehow or other terror must be met by greater terror,' wrote Sir Maurice Hankey, the Cabinet Secretary. And this is precisely what happened. When members of the new Dublin Castle administration met on 31 May to discuss the Irish situation with Lloyd George and Winston Churchill, the Minister for War, the new Chief Secretary complained of 'thugs' going about shooting people in Dublin, Cork and Limerick.

'We are certain that these are handsomely paid,' Greenwood said, 'the money comes from the USA.' According to him, Collins paid 'the murderers in public houses.'

'It is monstrous that we have 200 murders and no one hung,' Churchill cried. 'After a person is caught he should pay the penalty within a week. Look at the tribunals which the Russian government have devised. You should get three or four judges whose scope should be universal and they should move quickly over the country and do summary justice.' It was ironic that he, of all people, should privately advocate imitating the Bolshevik system, against which he railed in his public speeches.

'You agreed six or seven months ago that there should be hanging,' he said to Lloyd George.

'I feel certain you must hang,' the Prime Minister replied, but he doubted that an Irish jury would convict any rebel of a capital offence. In the circumstances, he therefore advocated economic pressure.

'Increase their pecuniary burdens,' he said. 'There is nothing farmers so much dislike as the rates'.

'Why not make life intolerable in a particular area?' Churchill asked.

'We are at present in very much of a fog,' Macready explained. The old system of intelligence had broken down, as the DMP's 'morale had been destroyed by the murders.' There was no longer an effective detective division in Ireland, though he added that a new system was being built.

While the British were re-organising, Collins' network was able to settle an old score. On 15 June Joe Sweeney happened to be in the bar of the Wicklow Hotel when Collins stomped in.

'We got the bugger, Joe.'

'What are you talking about?' Sweeney asked.

'Do you remember that first night outside the Rotunda? Lea Wilson?'

'I'll never forget it.'

'Well,' said Collins, 'we got him today in Gorey.'

He had tracked Wilson to Gorey, County Wexford, where he was an RIC District Inspector. He was shot dead that morning in revenge for his degrading treatment of Tom Clarke on the evening of the surrender in 1916.

'Sinn Féin has had all the sport up to the present, and we are going to have sport now,' Colonel Ferguson Smyth, the newly appointed RIC Divisional Commissioner for Munster, told the assembled police at the RIC station in Listowel on 19 June. A highly decorated veteran, he was scarred by the Great War in which he had been shot six times and had lost an arm as a result of his injuries. He seemed a rather embittered man as he advocated the RIC should shoot first and ask questions afterwards, but his remarks were obviously authorised because General Tudor was present.

'We must take the offensive and beat Sinn Féin at its own tactics,' Smyth said. 'If persons approaching carry their hands in their pockets or are suspicious looking, shoot them down. You may make mistakes occasionally, and innocent people may be shot, but that cannot be helped. No policeman will get into trouble for shooting any man.'

'By your accent I take it you are an Englishman, and in your ignorance you forget you are addressing Irishmen,' Constable Jeremiah Mee replied, appalled by the thought of such a policy.

He took off his cap and belt and threw them on a table.

'These too, are English,' he said. 'Take them.'

Smyth, a native of Banbridge, County Down, denied he was English. He ordered that Mee be arrested, but the constable's colleagues shared his indignation and ignored the order. Afterwards Mee drew up an account of what had happened and thirteen of those present testified to its accuracy by signing the statement.

Mee met Collins and others in Dublin on 15 July. Those present included the editor and managing director of the *Freeman's Journal*. For three hours Mee was questioned about the incident in Listowel. Naturally enough the *Freeman's Journal* covered the affair, much to the annoyance of the RIC, especially when Smyth was shot and killed on 18 July in the County Club in Cork city, where he had been traced by Collins' intelligence network.

'Were not your orders to shoot at sight?' his assassin asked. 'Well, you are in sight now, so prepare.'

The one-armed Smyth did not have a chance. He was shot some five times and died on the scene. When the authorities sought to hold an inquest afterwards, they were unable to find enough people to serve on a jury.

In the coming months, Collins would milk the controversy surrounding Smyth's remarks in Listowel for all the affair was worth in the propaganda war by recruiting Mee and two of his colleagues for speaking tours of the United States. In a way it was ironic because the policy advocated by Smyth was not really much different from that being pursued by the IRA in general, and Collins in particular. 'We may make mistakes in the beginning and shoot the wrong people,' Pearse had written in the article which Collins had endorsed so enthusiastically.

Collins' intelligence network also traced District Inspector Swanzy to Lisburn, County Antrim, where he was shot dead on 22 August in revenge for the killing of MacCurtain. 'Inspector Swanzy and his associates put Lord Mayor MacCurtain away,' Collins later explained, 'so I got Swanzy and all his associates wiped out, one by one, in all parts of the Ireland to which they had been secretly dispersed.'

IRA units in various parts of the country had begun attacking policemen, many on a mere random basis, as Breen and his colleagues had done at Soloheadbeg. One incident that caused particular revulsion was the killing of Constable Mulhern in

Bandon, County Cork. He was shot in the local Catholic Church, where he had gone to attend Sunday Mass on 25 July. Others were shot for no other reason than they were policemen, not because they had shown initiative against Sinn Féin or the IRA. When the Crown forces retaliated, it contributed to a vicious circle of violence.

Flying squads were established by the IRA in several areas to cope with the increasing mobility of Crown forces. Local leaders like Tom Barry and Liam Lynch in Cork, Tom Maguire in Mayo, and Seán MacEoin in the Longford area, generally acted independently of IRA headquarters, but Collins was always quick to endorse their actions, and this created the impression that their efforts were being orchestrated centrally. As a result Collins was often credited with, or accused of, involvement in skirmishes that he only learned about later.

Dick Mulcahy, for instance, looked on Breen and the Soloheadbeg gang as a kind of nuisance. Their wild, undisciplined approach to matters, especially their unauthorised killing of the two policemen on the day the Dáil was established, was resented. Even within the IRA, they were not generally welcome in Dublin. 'The only place in which they could find association and some kind of scope for their activities was on the fringe of Collins' Intelligence activity work,' according to Mulcahy.

Collins adopted a friendly attitude towards them. 'It would have been a comfort to them at all times compared with the natural attitude of Gearóid O'Sullivan and Diarmuid O'Hegarty,' Mulcahy wrote. Of course, Collins' 'rough breezy manner' afforded him 'greater flexibility in being able, while putting up with them when he liked, to get away with pushing them unceremoniously out of his way when he didn't want them.'

Lloyd George initial hope of using economic pressure to turn the Irish people against the rebels by putting the cost of fighting on the local rates was undermined when Sinn Féin won control of all but five of the island's 33 county councils in May 1920. As a result the party controlled the striking of rates throughout all but the north-east corner of Ireland. The following month Collins out-manoeuvred the British on the income tax front by getting the Dáil to establish a tax department.

All Irish people were called upon to 'pay income tax' to this new department rather than to the British government, and the Dáil promised to indemnify anyone against loss. The call was partly effective as people avoided Crown taxes by exploiting the chaos caused by the burning of tax offices in April. Some did pay the Sinn Féin regime, but most simply used the opportunity to evade income tax altogether.

With economic pressure holding little prospect for success, Lloyd George gave a virtually free rein to militants like Churchill and Greenwood. On 23 July Churchill told his cabinet colleagues 'it was necessary to raise the temperature of the conflict'. One of his pet schemes was to recruit 'a special force' of carefully selected men to act in Ireland. The cabinet authorised this during the summer, and advertisements were placed for a *Corps d'Elite* in which the recruits were supposed to be veteran officers from any of the services.

Known as Auxiliaries, they contained a mixture of fine men and scoundrels. On the whole they were more intelligent than the Black and Tans and received twice the pay. Like the Black and Tans they wore a blend of police and military uniforms with their own distinctive headgear, a Glengarry cap. They were heavily armed, each man carried two revolvers, some on low-slung holsters, wild west style, and they also had a rifle each, as well as a Sam Brown belt. They usually travelled in Crossley tenders, seated in two rows, sitting back-to-back, and they had at their disposal fast armoured cars with revolving turrets and Vickers machine guns. It made them a formidable force as far as the IRA was concerned. Although sometimes accused of having started the counter-terror, the policy was already in operation for some time before the Auxiliaries took up duty in September 1920.

During August the Black and Tans revenged attacks on their forces by 'shooting up' towns and burning the business premises or homes of people known to be sympathetic to Sinn Féin. In towns like Bantry, Fermoy, Thurles, Limerick, Enniscorthy, Tuam, and other towns and villages, they rampaged about the streets, shooting indiscriminately into buildings, and generally terrorising those communities. In the process nine civilians were killed.

Although a hardliner, Field Marshal Wilson was disgusted at the undisciplined conduct of the Black and Tans. 'I told Lloyd George that the authorities were gravely miscalculating the situation but he reverted to his amazing theory that someone was murdering two Sinn Féiners to every loyalist the Sinn Féiners were murdering,' Wilson wrote on 1 September. 'He seemed to be satisfied that a counter-murder association was the best answer to Sinn Féin murders.'

Collins, for his part, saw the British terror as a kind of mixed blessing, in that it clearly drove any doubting nationalists into the arms of Sinn Féin. 'The enemy continues to be savage and ruthless, and innocent people are murdered and outraged daily,' he wrote on 13 August. 'Apart from the loss which these attacks entail, good is done as it makes clear and clearer to people what both sides stand for.'

Even the DMP betrayed signs of uneasiness with British policy in the coming weeks. Since it was implicit in Collins' attitude towards the force that police would not be attacked if they stayed out of political or military matters, representatives of the DMP approached Sinn Féin for a guarantee that they would not be shot at if they stopped carrying weapons. Collins was consulted and he agreed, provided they also ceased their supportive role of the military on raids. The DMP commissioner agreed and the force was effectively withdrawn from the ongoing struggle during October.

While the terror and counter terror were spiralling, the British sent out peace feelers, and quietly orchestrated press speculation about a possible settlement on the lines of Dominion Home Rule. Fearing that Lloyd George was merely exploiting the speculation in order to obscure the terrorist policies of British forces, Collins tried to scotch the unfounded speculation by giving a newspaper interview to a celebrated American journalist. Carl Ackermann, who had earlier interviewed Lenin during the Russian revolution, had sought a meeting with Collins because the British considered him 'the most important member of the Irish Republican cabinet.'

'There will be no compromise,' Collins told Ackermann, 'and we will have no negotiations with any British government until Ireland is recognised as an independent Republic.'

'But Mr Collins,' the reporter asked, 'would you not consider accepting Dominion Home Rule as an instalment?'

'I see you think we have only to whittle our demand down to Dominion Home Rule and we shall get it. This talk about Dominion Home Rule is not promoted by England with a view to granting it to us, but merely with a view of getting rid of the Republican movement. England will give us neither as a gift. The same effort that would get us Dominion Home Rule will get us a Republic.'

Ackermann concluded his scoop with a prediction that 'there will be a real war in Ireland in the not-distant future.' A British officer told him 'the next few weeks will be decisive – one way or the other.'

At the time the Sinn Féin regime was clearly getting the better of the propaganda struggle on the world stage, and the movement received enormous publicity when the new Lord Mayor of Cork, Terence MacSwiney, went on hunger-strike to protest against his imprisonment. He had been arrested in August after being found in possession of police codes supplied by Collins. Although others were also on hunger-strike, he got the most extensive publicity because he was an elected member of the British parliament. His seventy-nine day fast was given worldwide publicity, and Lloyd George came under pressure from all sides to do something about MacSwiney and the deteriorating situation in Ireland.

Publicly he denied that British forces were killing people illegally, but in private he 'strongly defended the murder reprisals,' according to Sir Maurice Hankey, the Cabinet Secretary. 'The truth is that these reprisals are more or less winked at by the government.'

Winston Churchill became concerned that the security forces were 'getting out of control, drinking, and thieving, and destroying indiscriminately.' He argued that the reprisal policy should be formally regularised. Instead of turning a blind eye while the Black and Tans burned or killed indiscriminately, he wanted it done officially and publicly acknowledged, with the full support of the British government.

He wanted official hangings rather than shooting prisoners in cold blood and then contending they were killed while trying to escape. After months of clamouring he finally had his way on 1 November when Kevin Barry was hanged in Mountjoy Jail. He was an eighteen-year-old university student who had been captured after an IRA raid in which two British soldiers were killed. In view of his age, there was strong public pressure for his sentence to be commuted. Collins tried to arrange for Barry's escape but all efforts failed, and the young man became, in the words of the popular ballad:

> Another martyr for old Ireland,
> Another murder for the Crown,
> Whose brutal laws may kill the Irish
> But can't keep their spirit down.

With events in Ireland under the international spotlight, speculation about a possible settlement commanded growing press attention. The British had been sending out peace feelers ever since July when a Conservative member of parliament made discreet approaches to Art O'Brien, the Sinn Féin representative in London, about the kind of terms Sinn Féin would be looking for.

Collins was rather dismissive of the approach. He predicted that nothing was likely to develop unless the United States was asked to intervene or 'offered her services as a mediator.' Nevertheless Lloyd George continued to encourage peace feelers behind the scenes for the remainder of the year, through a number of people like John Steele of the *Chicago Tribune*, a Mayo businessman named Patrick Moylett, and George Russell (AE), the well-known writer. Peace speculation was boosted when former Prime Minister Asquith wrote to *The Times* in early October advocating that Britain offer Ireland 'the status of an autonomous Dominion in the fullest and widest sense.'

Moylett came to Dublin for informal talks with Griffith in mid-October, and, upon his return to London, was invited by Lloyd George to sit in on a Foreign Office meeting at which it was suggested that the Dáil should select three or four people to visit London for preliminary discussions about a formal conference to resolve the Irish situation.

Collins remained highly sceptical of the whole proceedings, and felt his suspicions were confirmed when Lloyd George declared in a major public address on 9 November that it was necessary to 'break the terror before you can get peace'. He left no doubt that he intended to pursue with his policy of counter-terror, and he seemed confident he was getting the upper hand.

'We have murder by the throat,' Lloyd George declared. 'We had to re-organise the police and when the government was ready we struck the terrorists and now the terrorists are complaining of terror.'

'I wonder what these people with their hypocritical good intentions and good wishes say to L. George's speech yesterday,' Collins wrote next day. 'So much for the peace feelers.'

9. 'The Destruction of the Undesirables'

Throughout most of 1920 Ireland was being infiltrated by British Secret Service agents intending to take on Collins and the IRA at their own game in line with the scenario outlined in the three-man committee on which Alan Bell had served. Most were recruited in London by Basil Thompson at Scotland Yard. They were known as the Cairo gang, because some of their more notorious hung out at the Cairo Cafe in Grafton Street.

Members of the gang lived in private houses and guest houses scattered around the city, and they were given passes to allow them to move about after curfew. McNamara furnished the names of people with curfew passes and by a process of elimination Collins' network was able to narrow the list down to likely agents.

Many of them stood out with English accents. They were 'mostly hoy hoy lah-di-dahs,' according to Brigadier General Frank Crozier, the commander of the Auxiliaries. Collins, with the help of his own agents in the postal sorting office, had the mail of suspected members of the Secret Service intercepted and delivered to himself.

Amidst the intercepted correspondence was a letter from Captain F. Harper Stove to Captain King on 2 March 1920. Even though the country was 'in a fearful mess,' Stove wrote that they should be able to put up 'a good show' because they had 'been given a free hand'.

'Re our little stunt,' he continued, 'there are possibilities.' In hindsight it became apparent that the killing of MacCurtain was part of their 'little stunt.'

The Secret Service planned to exterminate prominent members of Sinn Féin and make it appear that they had been killed in an IRA feud. They sent a threatening letter to MacCurtain on Dáil Éireann notepaper, seized the previous September in the raid on Sinn Féin headquarters.

'Thomas MacCurtain, prepare for death,' it read. 'You are doomed.'

In the following months most members of the Dáil received threatening letters. One was addressed to Collins at the Mansion House:

AN EYE FOR AN EYE.
A TOOTH FOR A TOOTH.
THEREFORE A LIFE FOR A LIFE.

'I'm quite safe,' Collins joked. 'If they get me, I'll claim I haven't received my death notice yet.'

While Collins made light of the threat on his own life, he took the overall threat posed by the Secret Service very seriously. In fact, he infiltrated it with at least one agent of his own. Willie Beaumont, a former British army officer, joined the Secret Service to spy for Collins. The agents from Britain had to rely on touts for information, and Beaumont pretended that members of Collins' intelligence staff – Cullen, Thornton, and Saurin – were his touts. He introduced them, and they got to know other Secret Service agents. On one occasion Cullen and Thornton were with Beaumont and Nelligan in a Grafton Street cafe when one of the Cairo gang joined them.

'Surely you fellows know these men – Liam Tobin, Tom Cullen and Frank Thornton,' he said. 'These are Collins' three officers, and if you can get them we could locate Collins himself.'

Getting Collins had clearly become a prime goal of the Secret Service, and they were getting close. At least they now knew the names of his staff, though they were seriously handicapped in not knowing what any of them looked like.

One of the British Secret Service agents, going under the name of F. Digby Hardy acted as a provocateur. He met Griffith and offered to set up his intelligence chief on Dun Laoghaire pier so that the IRA could kill him, but Collins was forewarned. Griffith invited reporters, including foreign correspondents, to a secret meeting on 16 September. Before the meeting he briefed them about Hardy.

'This man admits he is in the English Secret Service, and offered to arrange for the presence of the Secret Service Chief at a lonely point on Dun Laoghaire pier,' Griffith told the reporters. 'He asked me to let him meet leaders of the movement, especially on the military side, and he is coming here this evening imagining that he is to meet some inner council of the Sinn Féin movement. . . I will let him tell you his own story,' Griffith continued, 'but I will ask the foreign gentlemen present not to speak much lest the man's suspicion be aroused.'

Hardy duly arrived and told the gathering that he was a Secret Service agent and that upon his arrival in Ireland he had been met by Captain Thompson at Dun Laoghaire   pier and given instructions to find Michael Collins. He offered to arrange another meeting with Thompson on the pier so the IRA could kill him. He also said that he could arrange to lead the Auxiliaries into an ambush and could locate arsenals of the Ulster Volunteer Force. If the IRA could give him information about Collins' whereabouts, he said he would withhold the information for a couple of days and could then impress his Secret Service superiors by giving them the information.

'And, of course,' he added familiarly, 'no harm would come to Mick.'

'Well, gentlemen, you have heard this man's proposal and can judge for yourselves,' Griffith intervened. He then proceeded to expose Hardy as a convicted criminal, with actual details of his criminal record. 'You are a scoundrel, Hardy,' he said, 'but the people who employ you are greater scoundrels. A boat will leave Dublin tonight at 9 o'clock. My advice to you is – catch that boat and never return to Ireland.'

Griffith furnished the press with detailed inside information supplied by Collins about Hardy's criminal record. He had been freed from jail to work for the Secret Service, and it made for good propaganda to show that the British were using criminal elements to do their dirty work in Ireland. Indeed, the Sinn Féin Propaganda Department would do such an effective job that many Irish people believed the British had opened their jails for any criminals prepared to serve the Crown in Ireland. This was absurd, but incidents like the Hardy affair certainly lent it credence.

The following week the Secret Service struck again. John Lynch, a Sinn Féin County Councillor from Kilmallock, County Limerick, who had come to Dublin with National Loan Money for Collins, was shot dead in his room at the Exchange Hotel on the night of 23 September 1920. Secret Service agents claimed he had pulled a gun on them, but Collins dismissed this.

'There is not the slightest doubt that there was no intention whatever to arrest Mr Lynch,' he wrote. 'Neither is there the slightest doubt that he was not in possession of a revolver.'

Nelligan reported to Collins that Captain Bagalley, a one-legged courts martial officer had telephoned Dublin Castle about Lynch's presence in the hotel, and the men responsible for the actual shooting were two undercover officers using the names MacMahon and Peel, each a *nom de guerre*.

There was some suggestion that John Lynch was mistaken for Liam Lynch, an IRA commandant, but that was hardly likely seeing that there was an extreme difference in their ages. John Lynch was simply a Sinn Féiner and this had become a capital offence as far as the British Secret Service was concerned.

Griffith publicly charged the Secret Service with planning to kill moderates in Sinn Féin and give the impression that they were victims of an internal feud. In this way the movement's international support could be undermined. 'A certain number of Sinn Féin leaders have been marked down for assassination,' he said. 'I am first on the list. They intended to kill two birds with the one stone by getting me and circulating the story I have been assassinated by extremists because I am a man of moderate action.'

All British intelligence was being co-ordinated in Dublin Castle by Ormonde de L'Epée Winter. With his monocle and greased black hair plastered flat, he was like the prototype of a character in a spy thriller. 'A most amazing original' was how Assistant Secretary Mark Sturgis described him. 'He looks like a wicked little white snake, and is clever as pain, [and] probably entirely non-moral'.

In October Winter organised the Central Raid Bureau to co-ordinate the activities of his agents and the Auxiliaries. And they soon began to make their presence felt.

Major Gerald Smyth, a brother of the one-armed colonel shot in Cork on 18 July, had returned from the Middle East to avenge the death of his brother. It was rumoured that he had been killed by Dan Breen. So when Winter's people learned that Breen and Séan Tracy were spending the night of 11 October at the Drumcondra home of Professor John Carolan, Smyth was selected to lead the raiding party.

They burst into the house, but Smyth and a colleague were killed when Breen and Tracy shot blindly through their bedroom door before making a run for it. Although hit himself, Breen still managed to get away. He went up to a house at random and asked for help as he collapsed on the doorstep.

'I don't approve of gunmen,' he heard the man of the house

reply, 'I shall call the military.'

'If you do I'll report you to Michael Collins,' came a woman's voice from inside the house. The threat obviously worked because word was passed to the IRA and Breen was collected and taken to the Mater Hospital, where doctors and nurses colluded to hide his identity and the nature of his wounds.

Another patient was Professor Carolan whom the raiding party had put up against a wall and shot in the head; he died of his wounds but not before making a full death-bed statement about what had happened. Tracy had escaped unscathed from Drumcondra only to be shot dead a few days later.

Despite his busy schedule and the risk involved, Collins took a keen interest in Breen's recovery. He visited him in hospital and arranged his transfer to the home of Dr Alice Barry in the south side of the city as soon as he was ready to be moved. Breen was there about a week when he heard a commotion outside the house and looked out to find the whole block cordoned off by the Auxiliaries. They were searching the houses as a crowd of spectators gathered.

'I concluded there was no chance for me,' Breen wrote. 'As I surveyed the mass of spectators, I recognised the figure of Mick Collins.' He had seen the troops moving in the direction of the house and had followed them in case Breen needed to be rescued. As it was, the Auxiliaries did not bother to search Dr Barry's home, and Breen was spared.

At one point the DMP thought they had found Breen's body, so Sergeant Roche of the RIC was brought up from Tipperary to identify him. David Nelligan was given the gruesome task of accompanying Roche to the hospital morgue.

'That's not Dan Breen,' Roche said on being shown the body, 'I'd know his ugly mug anywhere.'

That evening Nelligan mentioned the incident to Liam Tobin and added that he was due to meet Roche on Ormonde Quay the following afternoon. To his horror next day, Nelligan found four members of the Squad waiting for Roche.

'For Christ's sake, what has he done?' Nelligan asked.

'I don't know,' one of the men replied. 'I've my orders to shoot him and that's what I'm going to do.'

Nelligan pleaded with them, but it was no good. They shot and killed Roche in front of him. A witness reported that he had seen Nelligan talking to one of the killers, and he had some difficulty extricating himself.

Nelligan was rightly annoyed that the incident had jeopard-
ised his cover as a spy. It really demonstrated a dangerous blind
spot in Collins' intelligence operations. As a man of action he
was so anxious to get things done that he sometimes acted
before the dust had settled to cover his agents' tracks. In early
October two American soldiers were shot and wounded by
Crown force in Queenstown (Cobh), and the Republican Publicity Bureau naturally exploited the incident in an effort to secure
American publicity and hopefully provoke some Anglo-American difficulties. Collins furnished the Republican Publicity Bureau with a copy of a report from General Tudor to Dublin Castle
suggesting that American sailors were engaged in smuggling
arms. The report had been supplied by McNamara, who was
called to the Commissioner's office and summarily dismissed
from the police force.

'You are lucky,' Collins told him. There was obviously no
hard evidence against McNamara, or he would not have been let
go so easily. Of course, Nelligan warned him that he still had to
be careful.

'Listen Mac,' he said, 'Don't go to your father's house tonight
or any night.'

There was a danger that he would be assassinated by the
Secret Service. He therefore went 'on the run' to work with the
Squad.

As of October 1920 the conflict had become extremely nasty.
Collins was deeply upset when he learned that the Black and
Tans had captured and tortured Tom Hales, a brother of his
closest friend in Frongoch. Another man tortured at the same
time went mad and had to be committed to a mental asylum.
Tom Hales managed to smuggle out an account of their ill-
treatment, which included pulling out his nails with pincers.

'I was with Collins when he received the message,' Piaras
Beaslaí recalled. 'He was beside himself with rage and pity, and,
as he told me afterwards, could not sleep that night for thinking
of it.' Collins himself wrote that the whole episode was something 'that no civilised nation can let pass unchallenged.' It was
ironic that he should have been so upset because Tom Hales was
the man who would organise the ambush to kill Collins at Beál
na mBláth less than two years later.

The torture of Hales was indicative of what Collins might
expect if he fell into enemy hand. He was now the most wanted
man in the country and the Cairo gang was getting close. 'We

were being made to feel that they were very close on the heels of some of us,' Mulcahy explained.

In the first two weeks of November they detained some of Collins' closest associates. They had Frank Thornton for ten days, but he managed to convince them that he had nothing to do with Sinn Féin. On the night of 10 November they just missed Mulcahy; he escaped out the skylight of Professor Michael Hayes' house in South Circular Road around five o'clock in the morning. Three days later they raided Vaughan's Hotel and questioned Liam Tobin and Tom Cullen, but they managed to bluff their way out of it. In a matter of three days the IRA's Chief-of-Staff and the three top men of Collins' intelligence network had been arrested and let go.

Collins prepared detailed files on suspected members of the Cairo gang. One of his sources – whom he merely referred to as 'Lt G,' helped identify the members of the gang. Collins planned on killing those he called 'the particular ones', and his spy suggested the coming Sunday morning as the best time to strike.

'Arrangements should now be made about the matter,' Collins wrote to McKee on 17 November. "Lt G" is aware of things. He suggests the 21st. A most suitable date and day I think.'

Although Collins was not always as careful as he should have been about protecting the identity of his spies, he was religious about keeping their names to himself. In this case 'Lt G' was apparently a woman typist at army headquarters. She always signed her notes to him with just the letter 'G', and he probably added the 'Lt' to make it more difficult for anyone to guess her identity. People naturally assumed his agent was an army officer.

On Saturday night Collins met with Brugha, Mulcahy, McKee and others to finalise arrangements in the headquarters of the printer's union at 35 Lower Gardiner Street, where the Dublin Brigade normally held meetings. Brugha felt there was insufficient evidence against some of those named by Collins. But there was no room for doubt in the cases of Peter Ames and George Bennett, the two men who had questioned Tobin and Cullen, nor with Captain Bagalley and the two men who had shot John Lynch at the Exchange Hotel, MacMahon and Peel. Brugha authorised their killings along with eleven others.

'It's to be done exactly at nine,' Collins insisted. 'Neither before nor after. These whores, the British, have got to learn that Irishmen can turn up on time.' The killings were to be a joint operation of the Squad and the Dublin Brigade, under the command of Dick McKee.

After the meeting Collins, McKee and some of the others went over to Vaughan's Hotel for a drink. There was a group of them in an upstairs room when Christy Harte, the porter, became suspicious of one of the hotel guests, a Mr Edwards, who had booked in three days earlier. He made a late night telephone call and then left the hotel, a rather ominous sign as it was after curfew. Harte immediately went upstairs to where Collins and the others were gathered.

'I think, sirs, ye ought to be going.'

Collins had come to trust Harte's instincts and had no hesitation now. 'Come on boys, quick,' he said, and all promptly headed for the door.

Collins took refuge a few doors down in the top floor flat of Dr Paddy Browne of Maynooth College at 39 Parnell Square. From there he watched the raid on Vaughan's Hotel a few minutes later. By then all the guests in the hotel were legitimately registered, with the exception of Conor Clune, a football supporter in Dublin for a game next day. He had come to the hotel with Peadar Clancy, and had apparently been forgotten. Clune was not registered. Although he was not a member of the IRA, he was obviously nervous when questioned because he made some rather inane comment about being prepared to die for Ireland, or something to that effect. He was therefore taken away for further questioning.

During the night McKee and Clancy were arrested where they were staying for the night, but everything was already in train for the morning. Eleven different assassination teams took part. Some used church bells, and others waited for clocks to strike before they began the operations, exactly at nine o'clock. Each team contained a member of the Squad as well as an Intelligence Officer, assigned to search the bodies and rooms for documents.

Eleven of the Cairo Gang were shot and killed at eight different locations, some in the presence of their families. Captain W.F. Newbury's pregnant wife was in the room with him at the time; the following week their child was still-born. There was some confusion over whether or not Captain MacCormack of the Royal Army Veterinary Corps was on the list. He was shot dead in the Gresham Hotel, but Collins had no evidence against him. 'We have no evidence he was a Secret Service agent,' he later wrote. 'Some of the names were put on by the Dublin

Brigade.' This, of course, raised some questions about the clinical efficiency with which the attacks were supposedly carried out.

Also killed were two Auxiliaries who just happened to be passing the scene of one of the killings at 22 Lower Mount Street as the gunmen were trying to escape while a maid was screaming hysterically from an upstairs window. One of Lynch's killers had been shot there but his colleague managed to escape by barricading himself in his room while some twenty shots were fired into the door. Frank Teeling of the Dublin Brigade was captured by Auxiliaries.

General Crozier, the commander of the Auxiliaries, was nearby and he visited the house on Mount Street. He then went to Dublin Castle to report what had happened. While there, word was received by telephone of the other killings.

'What!' the officer who answered the telephone exclaimed, turning deathly pale. He staggered as he turned around after hanging up and had to clutch a table for support.

'About fifty officers are shot in all parts of the city,' he said, 'Collins has done in most of the secret service people.'

'In Dublin Castle panic reigned. For the next week the gates were choked with incoming traffic – all military, their wives and agents,' according to Nelligan. One distraught agent whose pals had been killed, shot and killed himself and was buried with the others in England, where they were given a state funeral, with services at Westminster Abbey.

Collins certainly had no regrets about what he had organised. 'My own intention was the destruction of the undesirables who continued to make miserable the lives of ordinary decent citizens,' he wrote. 'I have proof enough to assure myself of the atrocities which this gang of spies and informers have committed. Perjury and torture are words too easily known to them.' If he had another motive, he added, 'it was no more than a feeling such as I would have for a dangerous reptile.'

'That should be the future's judgment on this particular event,' he wrote. 'For myself my conscience is clear. There is no crime in detecting and destroying in war-time, the spy and the informer. They have destroyed without trial. I have paid them back in their own coin.'

'The attack was so well organised, so unexpected, and so ruthlessly executed that the effect was paralysing,' according to Nelligan. 'It can be said that the enemy never recovered from the blow. While some of the worst killers escaped, they were thoroughly frightened.'

Two of those who escaped were Captain King and Lieutenant Hardy, who were particularly despised by the IRA because of their brutal treatment of prisoners; they were not in their residences when the hit-teams called. Todd Andrews of the Dublin Brigade burst into King's room to find only his half-naked mistress. Shocked by the sudden intrusion, she sat bolt upright in bed and looked terror-stricken.

'I felt a sense of shame and embarrassment for the woman's sake,' Andrews noted, but the two Squad members with him were too frustrated at missing King to have any sympathy for the unfortunate woman.

'I was so angry I gave the poor girl a right scourging with the sword scabbard,' Joe Dolan recalled. 'Then I set the room on fire.'

Andrews was horrified at the conduct of Dolan and the other Squad member. They 'behaved like Black and Tans,' he noted.

Hardy and King, on the other hand, gave vent to their rage by torturing and then killing McKee, Clancy, and Clune in Dublin Castle.

Elsewhere in the city the Auxiliaries went on a rampage at Croke Park, where they raided a football game and began firing indiscriminately into the crowd. Twelve innocent people, including one of players on the field, were killed and scores wounded. They claimed that they were fired upon, as British soldiers would contend on another bloody Sunday some fifty years later, but Crozier publicly refuted the claim afterwards.

'It was the most disgraceful show I have ever seen,' one of his officers told him. 'Black and Tans fired into the crowd without any provocation whatever.'

In London Lloyd George and members of the cabinet were very jittery, according to Sir Maurice Hankey. Greenwood provided weapons for all his domestic staff, though – unlike the Prime Minister – he was able to joke about his own predicament.

'All my household are armed,' the Chief Secretary told the cabinet, 'my valet, my butler, and my cook. So if you have any complaints about the soup you may know what to expect.'

There was good reasons to be fearful. Brugha, it will be remembered, had raised a force to go into the House of Commons and kill as many members of the government as possible if conscription had been enforced in 1918, and he would resurrect this plan in the coming weeks.

Other arrangements were already made for a large scale operation in Britain, where the IRA planned incendiary attacks on warehouses in the Liverpool and Manchester areas. On the day after Bloody Sunday Collins wanted to send an important message to the IRA in Britain and he arranged for Jeremiah Mee, who had been working for Countess Markievicz since his resignation from the RIC over the late Colonel Smyth's remarks in Listowel, to take the message personally. He was selected because he had a military look about him, but Mee had been trying to conceal this.

'What happened to your little moustache?' Collins asked.

Mee explained he shaved it off because the Countess thought it looked too military.

'Be damn to her,' cried Collins, 'she should know by now that a military appearance is the best disguise for our men at the present time.'

He proceeded to outline the best way for Mee to behave in order to avoid detection. The advice provided a real insight into how Collins had been able to move about Dublin so freely in recent months. Dress up in spats with good creases on his pants and carrying a walking stick and a supply of cigars, he told Mee.

'Get into friendly chat with some of the military officers,' he added. 'You can do this by passing round your cigars and even if they do not smoke cigars it will at least be an introduction and will save you being questioned or searched. That is how I get across myself and you should have no difficulty if you keep your head screwed on.'

Collins might well have gone himself except that he was anxious to pay his last respects to McKee and Clancy. Their deaths had been a terrible blow to his morale. They were 'two men who fully understood the inside of Collins' work and his mind, and who were ever ready and able to link up their resources of the Dublin Brigade to any work that Collins had in hand, and to do so promptly, effectively and sympathetically,' Mulcahy noted.

He was so upset by their deaths that he seemed to become quite reckless. He not only went to the cathedral to dress the bodies in IRA uniforms, but also took a prominent part in the funeral. At one point he was actually filmed as he stepped out of the crowd to lay a wreath on the grave. Attached was a note signed by himself: 'In memory of two good friends – Dick and Peadar – and two of Ireland's best soldiers.'

As he stepped forward to the grave, he overheard a woman. 'Look,' she said, 'there's Michael Collins.'

He turned and glared at her. 'You bloody bitch,' he snarled.

Given his state of mind, it was a measure of his respect for Griffith that he was still ready to go along with Lloyd George's continuing peace feelers, even though he had no faith in them himself.

Moylett had visited Dublin again in November and brought a letter from Griffith to the Prime Minister on the eve of Bloody Sunday. One might have thought the events of the next day would have killed the peace initiative at this point, but not at all. When Moylett met Lloyd George next day, the Prime Minister did not seem unduly perturbed.

'They got what they deserved,' Lloyd George supposedly said.

That, at any rate, was Moylett's story, but Art O'Brien, the Sinn Féin representative in London, warned Collins that the Mayo man was just a 'Big-Blower' and a damn fool.

'Your view is shared by me,' Collins replied, 'but Mr Griffith thinks differently, therefore, I am keeping in touch with this man for the present.'

While Moylett was meeting with Lloyd George, Steele was talking with Griffiths about a possible ceasefire on both sides. 'I'll do all I can [to] stop murders but you must call off reprisals at the same time,' was Griffith's message for the Prime Minister.

Lloyd George met the Irish writer George Russell (AE) on 26 November and told him that he would negotiate with anybody but Collins and somebody called 'Gallagher.' Presumably the Prime Minister was referring to Mulcahy, and either he or Russell got the name mixed up. Lloyd George's message to Russell was basically that he would call off military operations if there were three weeks of peace. Then negotiations could begin, though he indicated there were limits as to what the British would consider.

'We will not tolerate a Republic,' he emphasised, 'but anything short of that.'

Whatever hope Lloyd George entertained for his proposals was seriously upset that day by the arrest of Griffith, who had been picked up in a nationwide swoop of Sinn Féin supporters. As a result Collins took over as acting President.

10. 'Get On With Our Work'

Collins was acting President for four hectic weeks, amid a welter of peace rumours, some of the bloodiest fighting, the most widespread round up of suspects since the Easter Rebellion, and the movement of the campaign to Britain for the first time.

'Those of us who were in constant touch with him always possessed the fear that he would collapse under it,' Ó Muirthile wrote. Now those fears became all the more real when Collins – still deeply upset over the brutal killings of McKee and Clancy – assumed the extra strain of the Presidency.

He was not even in his new post two full days when the British-based IRA fire-bombed more than a dozen warehouses in the Liverpool docks area, causing millions of pounds worth of damage. That same day in Kilmichael, County Cork, Tom Barry led an IRA ambush on a convoy of Auxiliaries and killed seventeen of them. The Kilmichael attack raised Collins' spirits immediately.

'Good man Barry!' he exclaimed on hearing the news.

Lloyd George, who had clearly intimated that British forces were coming to grips with things in Ireland when he proudly boasted of having 'murder by the throat', was now faced with irrefutable evidence that the rebels were far from finished. The last full week of November was, in fact, the bloodiest in Ireland since 1916.

On 1 December Lloyd George opened up a new peace channel, this time through the Irish-born Roman Catholic Archbishop of Perth, Australia, Patrick J. Clune. He asked him to meet the Irish leaders in Dublin and sound them out about negotiations and a possible ceasefire.

Griffith, who met the archbishop in Mountjoy Jail, advised Collins against a meeting because of the danger that British agents were watching Clune, but then Collins met him without difficulty on 4 December at a school run by Louise Gavan Duffy on St Stephen's Green.

Even if the Secret Service were keeping an eye on the archbishop, they would have considered his visit to her school quite natural as she was a daughter of Sir Charles Gavan Duffy, a former Young Ireland leader who had risen to the top in Australian politics having migrated there in the mid-nineteenth century.

'I wonder how it is that the archbishop sees Collins apparently without difficulty in Dublin and our intelligence fails to find him after weeks of search,' Mark Sturgis wrote in obvious exasperation.

Collins gave Clune a written outline of ceasefire terms agreeable to the Dáil cabinet. 'If it is understood that the acts of violence (attacks, counter-attacks, reprisals, arrests, pursuits) are called off on both sides,' he wrote, 'we are agreeable to issue the necessary instructions on our side, it being understood that the entire Dáil shall be free to meet and that its peaceful activities be not interfered with.'

Before the archbishop could return to Britain, a figurative spanner was thrown in the works when some Sinn Féin members of Galway county council called publicly for peace talks, and Father Michael O'Flanagan, the Sinn Féin Vice-President, wrote to Lloyd George suing for peace terms. Although both acts were unauthorised, Collins realised their significance immediately. He asked the secretary of the party to inform the press 'that Father O'Flanagan acted without any authority from the Sinn Féin Standing Committee, and without consulting that body. . . We must not allow ourselves to be rushed by these foolish productions, or foolish people, who are tumbling over themselves to talk about a "truce," when there is no truce,' Collins wrote.

The *Irish Independent* suggested a hitch had developed in secret talks because of the difficulty in organising a truce in which Collins' safety could be assured. He forcefully denied the report and lashed out against the recent unauthorised overtures in a short letter to the newspaper's editor.

'My personal safety does not matter and does not count as a factor in the question of Ireland's right,' he explained. 'I thank no one for refraining from murdering me. At the moment there is a very grave danger that the country may be stampeded on false promises and foolish ill-timed actions. We must stand up against that danger. My advice to the people is, "Hold fast".'

People in the movement were rushing 'to talk of truce' when there was no indication the British were ready to call off their aggression, he complained in another letter to the press. As far as he was concerned, the Irish side was merely acting in self-defence. 'If the aggression ceases there will be no longer any need

for defence,' he argued. 'But is the aggression ceasing? Every-
where the enemy has gone on with his attack,' Collins added,
answering his own question. 'Let us drop talking and get on with
our work.'

'Everyone in Ireland has reason to be profoundly distrustful of
British politicians of all schools, and we have learned to be more
distrustful of their promises than of their threats,' he continued.
'Prepare to meet their threats, but let their promises be
realised.Then, we can bestow thanks according to value.'

His scepticism was well-founded. When Clune returned to
London, he found Lloyd George's attitude had stiffened. Pass-
ions were so roused over the recent killings, the Prime Minister
said, it was necessary to hold off on actual talks for a while
longer. If the Irish would keep things quiet for about a month, he
predicted the atmosphere would be more conducive for negotiations. He also added it would help matters if Collins and
Mulcahy left the country for a while. The archbishop concluded
the British attitude had changed because they believed
O'Flanagan's letter and the telegram from the six members of
the Galway County Council were indications Sinn Féin was
'showing the white feather'. Clune heard the Prime Minister
call a meeting with his hardliners, and it was noteworthy that
when Lloyd George spoke in parliament afterwards, he said the
'extremists must first be broken up' before there could be a
negotiated settlement, and he announced the introduction of
martial law throughout the southern counties of Ireland.

Next evening the Black and Tans and Auxiliaries ran amuck
in Cork, burning much of the business centre of the city in a
frightening rampage of arson and looting. The outcry was such
that the government ordered a formal military inquiry.

When Clune returned to Mountjoy for further discussions
with Griffith on 12 December, Collins was clearly disillusioned.
'It seems to me that no additional good result can come from
further continuing these discussions,' he wrote to Griffith. 'We
have clearly demonstrated our willingness to have peace on honourable terms. Lloyd George insists upon capitulation. Between
these there is no mean, and it is only a waste of time continuing.'

Collins was afraid that their willingness to continue with
such talks might be interpreted in Britain as an indication that
the Irish side was desperate for peace because it was on the verge
of collapse. 'Let Lloyd George make no mistake,' Collins continued, 'the IRA is not broken.'

Although Lloyd George's coalition government had been given a handsome majority in the last general election, his own political position was really precarious because his Liberal Party had been decimated at the polls, and the Conservative Party, with which he was in coalition, had won an overwhelming majority of its own within Westminster. Thus the Prime Minister was really a political prisoner of the Conservatives who traditionally tended to take a hardline on Irish matters.

Clune was convinced Lloyd George was 'genuinely anxious' for a settlement and was being hampered by diehards in his government, but their position had been weakened by the recent outrageous behaviour of Crown forces. 'The Cork burnings have strengthened his hands against the diehards,' the archbishop argued. In addition, there was also the senseless killing of a Catholic priest, Canon Magner. He had been shot in Cork by the Black and Tans after he had stopped to help a local magistrate who was having car trouble. 'His sole offence was to have helped a Resident Magistrate to get his motor car going, and here comes a drunken beast of a soldier who makes him kneel down and shoots him,' Lloyd George told his cabinet.

Griffith tended to agree with Clune about the Prime Minister's desire for a settlement. 'He apparently wants peace, but is afraid of his militarists,' he wrote to Collins.

All this was 'being too credulous of Lloyd George's intentions,' as far as Collins was concerned. 'My own feeling about Lloyd George is that we should not allow him to disassociate himself from his public actions, as Head of his cabinet, and from the actions resulting from decisions of his cabinet,' Collins wrote to Art O'Brien on 15 December. 'Particularly on this side, there is far too great a tendency to believe that Lloyd George is wishful for peace, and that it is only his own wild men prevent him from accomplishing his desires.'

Nevertheless the archbishop now brought proposals from Dublin Castle that the British were willing to stop arrests, raids, or reprisals for a month in return for a ceasefire on the Irish side, but they were not prepared to agree formally that the Dáil should be allowed to meet. It was not that they wanted to prevent such meetings but rather they did not want to be seen to be formally approving of them.

'A truce on the terms specified cannot possibly do us any harm,' Collins wrote to Griffith. He had consulted Brugha and Stack and both were agreeable. Stack was ready to accept if

Collins was, while Brugha merely insisted that 'it must be definitely understood that our peaceful activities are not to be interfered with.'

Just as everything seemed ready for a truce, the British again scuttled the process. Clune returned to Griffith on 17 December with news that Dublin Castle was now insisting that the IRA should first surrender its arms. This, of course, was tantamount to demanding capitulation, and Griffith told him without hesitation that it would not even be considered.

Next day Collins met Clune for a second time. 'Our interview was not a lengthy one,' Collins wrote. 'We had both, practically speaking, come to the conclusion that no talk was necessary, seeing that the new proposal from the British government was a proposal that we should surrender.'

A number of factors contributed to Lloyd George's change of heart, but in the last analysis the main reason was unwillingness to confront his cabinet hardliners, who were predicting that they were on the verge of victory. 'Stress was laid on on the importance of doing nothing to check the surrender of arms at a time when the forces of the Crown had at last definitely established the upper hand,' the Cabinet Secretary noted in his diary.

The talk about getting the upper hand was strengthened by the antics of Father O'Flanagan and six members of Galway County Council clamouring for peace, followed by the bitter denunciation of ambushes by the Roman Catholic Bishop of Cork, Daniel Cohalan, who announced the excommunication of anyone engaging in ambushes.

'Anyone who shall within the Diocese of Cork, organise or take part in an ambush or in a kidnapping, or otherwise shall be guilty of murder or attempt at murder,' the bishop said, 'shall incur by the very fact the censure of excommunication.'

'That is pretty serious,' Lloyd George noted. He saw the sermon as an indication that the hierarchy were turning away from Sinn Féin.

On top of all this the British had their own intelligence reports that de Valera was on his way back from the United States, and they believed that he would be easier to deal with than a militant like Collins. As things stood Clune told the British that Collins was 'the only one with whom business could be done,' but they gave the archbishop the impression that they thought O'Flanagan and de Valera would be more ready to compromise.

The British cabinet was told on 20 December that de Valera would be landing at Liverpool that day and Lloyd George suggested that no effort should be made to arrest him.

'I cannot guarantee de Valera's safety now,' Greenwood declared.

'That is his look out,' the Prime Minister replied.

'How can you let de Valera loose when we have arrested Arthur Griffith?' Greenwood asked.

'That was a piece of impertinence on the part of the military and if it had not been for the fact that we want support of the military we would have repudiated it,' Lloyd George explained.

The Clune talks were only one of the things that Collins had to concern himself with during his month as acting President. In addition to being acting President of the Dáil, he was still Minister for Finance, President of the IRB, and Director of Intelligence in the IRA.

He was really an administrative genius, able to compartmentalise all matters and keep them separate, while at the same time slicing through bureaucratic red tape. He believed in getting right to the heart of a matter and balked at the paper shuffling in which civil servants often spend so much of their time.

'Look here,' he wrote to the Cabinet Secretary, Diarmuid O'Hegarty, 'I am not going to have any more of the parcels of miscellanies dumped on me. If anything concerns this department, or the general aspect, it should be sent to me and no more about it – I have something else to do than to wade through a miscellaneous collection of cuttings, surmounted by a letter from the Propaganda Department to you, a letter from you to the Propaganda Department, and another letter to myself. If a little common sense is applied, the situation will be very much simplified,' he declared.

He had the neat, orderly mind of a trained civil servant. He liked his reports typed, or at least written in ink. 'For God's sake,' he wrote to one Intelligence Officer in the habit of sending pencilled reports, 'buy a pen and a bottle of ink.'

Collins returned an illegible report to another officer. 'What in Heaven's name is the use of mystifying me with a thing like this?' he asked.

His own letters were a model of businesslike clarity – short and to the point, with numbered paragraphs for different items, and separate letters dealing with intelligence and financial matters.

His good friend Harry Boland used to irritate him by including Sinn Féin, IRB, and personal matters in the same letters, which caused problems, if Collins wished to pass on the letters to someone else. But try as he might, there was no way some people would adopt the kind of reporting habits Collins wanted.

'I undertook to fight for you, not to write for you,' Seán MacEoin snapped back in irritation one day.

'Got plenty of staff, Austin?' Collins asked one day on entering the office of Austin Stack, the Minister for Home Affairs.

'Yes,' replied the Kerryman.

'Well I have just received the following,' Collins snarled, dumping a bundle of complaints on his desk. 'Your department, Austin, is nothing but a bloody joke.'

The rather sensitive Stack resented the remark. A few days later when someone referred to Collins as the Big Fellow, Stack betrayed bitterness.

'Big Fella!' he said. 'He's no Big Fella to me.'

The nickname born of derision, had become a term of affection, but there was no longer any affection between Collins and Stack. Their once warm friendship was rapidly developing into an extremely bitter rivalry in which Collins made no effort to spare the personal feelings of Stack, whom he would come to despise.

Pádraic O'Keeffe, who served with Stack as Joint National Secretary of Sinn Féin, noted it was 'easy to work with' him. 'Of course,' O'Keeffe added pointedly, 'he did no work.'

Despite a reputation for interfering in the affair of colleagues, Collins would have been quite content to let Stack alone if he had been working properly, but the Kerryman had never been able to get on top of his job. And then he antagonised Collins by transmitting routine material though the IRA's express communications network. It was a kind of 'fastrack' service in which railway men carried sensitive IRA messages all over the country. Collins had set up the network and was very protective of it. He would not have minded it being used for something important, but resented Stack endangering the process just to transmit routine stuff.

Collins 'never crossed the boughs of anybody who was doing work and particularly anybody in authority,' according to Mulcahy. This was undoubtedly an exaggeration, but it was particularly significant coming from the IRA Chief-of-Staff, who noted that Collins 'set himself out to serve unreservedly in every possible way.' He certainly had an excellent working relationship with Griffith, during the period of the latter's acting Presidency.

Collins was a demanding task-master, always pushing and shoving to get things done. He pushed everyone, especially himself. Throughout the movement people looked to him for action.

'There was no burden too big to put on Mick's shoulders, and there was no job too small for him to do,' according to Dan Breen.

'Whenever anybody wanted anything done they were told to see Mick,' Tom Barry noted. 'He was very good-hearted and generous, but he was also a man you could easily dislike. He was very domineering.'

Witnesses were often embarrassed by the way Collins bullied his aide Joe O'Reilly. The latter was everything to him, confidant, messenger, nurse, sometimes body-guard, and the person who bore the brunt of the Big Fellow's rages when he let off steam as things went wrong, which was quite often for a perfectionist like Collins. They had been friends since their emigrant days in London, and O'Reilly was a perfect sidekick – totally devoted to Collins, though at times the bullying did get to him. O'Reilly would announce he was leaving, and Collins would act indifferently, making no effort to change his friend's mind.

'Here!' Collins would say. 'Take this letter on your way.'

'Do you know what you're doing to that boy?' one woman asked Collins in disgust.

'I know his value better than you do,' he replied. 'He goes to Mass for me every morning. Jesus Christ, do you think I don't know what he's worth to me?'

O'Reilly always returned, of course, because in spite of everything he knew that Collins valued his services. Maybe the reason Collins would not ask him to stay was his recognition that nobody should be pressed to take the risks that O'Reilly took for him. Collins, in turn, trusted him with his very life, because O'Reilly always knew where to find Collins; he was the only person who knew where Collins was sleeping on any given night.

Finding a bed for the night was usually a problem for someone like Collins. The Munster Hotel was the subject of regular raids, so it was too dangerous for him to stay there throughout 1920, and Vaughan's Hotel became much too dangerous after Bloody Sunday. People putting him up at night had to be particularly brave because they were endangering their own lives and those of their families. He often stayed at the Rathgar home of Mrs O'Donovan, an aunt of Gearóid O'Sullivan, or on Richmond Avenue in Walter House, the home of a colleague's widowed mother. Collins had digs in Walter House for a time before moving to the Munster Hotel. He also stayed at 23 Brendan's Road with his secretary Susan Mason and her aunt, or with Patricia Hoey and her mother at 5 Mespil Road in the house where he had his intelligence office. Another of his safe houses was Furry Park, the home of Moya Llewelyn Davies. She was the daughter of James O'Connor, a late Parnellite member of parliament, and her husband was a confidant of Lloyd George. With credentials like those, her home was one of the last places the security forces were likely to raid.

Nobody suggested then there was anything sexual between Collins and any of those women. At the time he did not show any interest in the opposite sex. Given his lifestyle and his precarious prospects, it was understandable that he should have avoided entangling relationships. Later people would suggest that there might have been something more to his relationship with some of those women, but nobody ever produced a shred of evidence to substantiate their snide insinuations, or in some cases actual accusations. About all one can say at this juncture was that if Collins was having an affair at the time, he was certainly discreet.

On the evening of de Valera's return to Ireland, Collins arranged a party with some friends in the Gresham Hotel. The attendance, which was exclusively male, included Rory O'Connor, Gearóid O'Sullivan, Liam Tobin, Tom Cullen, and himself. He also invited David Nelligan, his spy in Dublin Castle, but Nelligan declined.

'Dave's getting windy,' Collins exclaimed.

During the evening the hotel was raided by the Auxiliaries, and all were questioned and searched.

'What is your name?' the Auxiliary officer asked Collins.

'John Grace.'

'What is your job?'

'I am an accountant.'

'Where do you work?'

'My office is in Dame Street.'

Collins had an ordnance survey map in his possession with the words 6 refills written in a corner. The officer suggested it said rifles, but the neat handwriting left little room for confusion.

'They were very suspicious of me,' Collins told friends next day. 'I was questioned over and over again. The officer actually drew an old photograph of me out of his pocket, and compared it with my face, drawing my hair down as it was in the picture. It was touch and go. They were not quite satisfied, and hesitated long before they left us.'

Throughout it all Collins remained cheerful, and the raiding party eventually departed, leaving him to get very drunk indeed.

Afterwards they went to Vaughan's hotel. Cullen left to get a car, and Beaslaí arrived to find O'Sullivan sprawled on a chair, while O'Connor and Collins were embracing themselves on the floor.

11. 'That Long Whore Won't Get Rid of Me as Easy as That'

Although he tried to persuade de Valera not to go to the United States, Collins nevertheless arranged through his Liverpool contacts to have him and Harry Boland smuggled to America. And he was delighted with their welcome on the other side of the Atlantic, though he was critical of the two of them for talking too much about their respective trips.

'You should not be so communicative over there,' Collins wrote to Boland on 19 July. 'Other people may want to go in the same manner.'

Being New York-born de Valera attracted a considerable amount of press attention, and a crowd of some 50,000 people crammed into Fenway Park, Boston, to hear him on the first stop of a speaking tour. Instead of his proper title – *Priomh Aire* (Prime Minister) of Dáil Éireann – he described himself as President of the Irish Republic, a title that afforded him a more impressive platform from which to appeal to Americans. Initially he was afraid his unauthorised adoption of the new title might be resented in some quarters at home. The IRB had always claimed that title for the head of its supreme council, but Collins, who was selected to the post about this time, certainly had no objections. Indeed, he referred quite matter-of-factly to de Valera as 'the President' in a letter to his IRB colleague, Stack, on 20 July: 'The President is getting tremendous receptions and the press in its entirety has thrown itself open to Irish propaganda.' He not only accepted de Valera as a legitimate successor to Pearse, but also basically recognised that the Dáil had a legitimate line from the IRB's Fenian movement. He advocated the Dáil should honour Fenian bonds, but de Valera had insisted on the exclusion of a reference to the Fenian bonds in the prospectus for the new bonds. When he went to the United States, however, de Valera changed his mind and publicly endorsed the suggestion, thereby prompting Collins to write to him rather tactlessly, that 'it was worth going to America to be converted to that idea.'

The remark was a mere passing comment, but to someone like de Valera, for whom every written word was carefully calculated, the whole thing was pregnant with significance.

'What did you mean it was worth going to America to be "converted" to the idea of paying the Fenian bonds?' he asked indignantly. 'Surely I never opposed acknowledging that as a National debt. You must mean something else. What is it?'

'I meant about the Fenian bonds, that it was worth going to America to be converted to my idea,' Collins replied. 'Honestly I did not think the fact that I was practically forced to delete a certain paragraph from the prospectus looked much in favour of the idea. For God's sake, Dev, don't start an argument about its being from the prospectus only, etc. Don't please. It's quite all right.'

De Valera had planned to sell Republican bonds as soon as possible in the United States, but he ran into legal difficulties, and it took some six months before he could get the whole thing sorted out and off the ground. Collins, on the other hand, was in the happier position of not having to bother with legal niceties, and he launched the National Loan in Ireland during August 1919.

After he got the programme underway, he was asked to come to the United States to help de Valera, but he believed his place was at home. While he realised America could play both a financial and a propaganda role in helping Ireland, Collins was convinced this would only happen if the requests for help were warranted by actual events in Ireland.

'Our hope is here and must be here,' he wrote. 'The job will be to prevent eyes turning to Paris or New York as a substitute for London.' In short, they should not make the mistake of getting too caught up in efforts to secure international recognition because, in the last analysis, they could only win by wearing down the British government.

James O'Mara, one of the trustees of the Dáil, went to the United States instead of Collins and took over the organisation of a bond-certificate drive. As the Irish Republic had not been officially recognised, it would have been illegal to sell bonds, but, with the help of Judge Daniel Cohalan of the New York Supreme Court, the law was circumvented by selling certificates entitling purchasers to buy bonds of a similar value once the Irish Republic was recognised.

A bitter political feud developed in the United States after the leaders of Clan na Gael – Cohalan and John Devoy, the editor of the *Gaelic American* – accused de Valera of interfering in American affairs, and he charged them with trying to dictate on purely Irish affairs. As elected leader of the Irish people, he felt he should have the final say in speaking for Ireland, whereas they felt they should have the last word in matters relating to the United States. He angered them by campaigning publicly on the question of American ratification of the' Versailles Treaty to which they were unalterably opposed. His message, on the other hand, was that if President Wilson recognised the Irish Republic's right to membership of the League of Nations, then 'Irishmen and men and women of Irish blood will be behind him'. In short, de Valera was presuming to speak for Irish-Americans and committing them to something that was totally unacceptable to Devoy and Cohalan.

Their simmering differences only became public, however, when Devoy attacked de Valera over remarks made during an interview with a correspondent of the *Westminster Gazette* in February 1920. Believing that American politicians were loath to recognise the Irish Republic because an independent Ireland would pose a threat to Britain (their ally in the recent Great War), de Valera tried to placate this fear by suggesting a kind of English Monroe Doctrine for the British Isles. He said Ireland would guarantee that her territory would never be used against Britain, and he proposed an Anglo-Irish treaty on the lines of the Cuban-American Treaty of 1901.

Devoy was critical of the use of the Cuban treaty as a model for Anglo-Irish relations because some of its aspects impinged on Cuba's sovereignty, and such a treaty would commit Ireland to supporting Britain in the event of an Anglo-American war. The arguments were valid from a purely academic standpoint, but de Valera over-reacted to the criticism by attacking Cohalan who, he somehow believed, was responsible for the *Gaelic American* editorial.

'Big as this country is,' de Valera wrote to Griffith, 'it is not big enough to hold the judge and myself.' He was actually so tactless as to repeat his statement to a meeting of prominent Irish-Americans. The Catholic bishop of Buffalo, who was chairing the meeting, remarked that Cohalan could hardly be expected 'to leave his native land just because the President had decided to come.'

A political truce was agreed at the meeting. Clan na Gael

promised to keep out of purely Irish matters, and de Valerá agreed to stay out of American affairs, but he had no intention of honouring his pledge. Immediately after the meeting, for instance, he asked the Dáil to authorise him secretly to spend up to a quarter of a million dollars on the forthcoming American elections.

De Valera's critics were by no means confined to a Clan na Gael clique, as has sometimes been suggested. Patrick MacCartan was an outspoken critic of Cohalan and Devoy, but he nevertheless noted at the time that de Valera had been needlessly antagonising people by betraying 'an unconscious contempt' for the views of others. He wrote that the President 'tends to force his own opinions without hearing from the other fellows and thus thinks he has co-operation when he only gets silent acquiescence.' James O'Mara, the man sent out by Collins to organise the loan programme, resigned over de Valera's highhanded actions.

'What on earth is wrong with Mr O'Mara?' Collins wrote to Boland. 'There always seems to be something depressing coming from the USA.' O'Mara agreed to continue following an appeal from Griffith warning that his resignation would be damaging to the movement. Some months later, however, he again resigned because he had 'no longer any confidence' in de Valera's judgment of American affairs, and he resented de Valera's assumption of 'arbitrary executive authority'.

There was uneasiness in Dublin over the stance taken by de Valera in the *Westminster Gazette* interview. Fr O'Flanagan wrote to Collins complaining about the 'suspicion that we were prepared to desert our friends in a foolish attempt to placate our enemies. In the last resort,' O'Flanagan insisted, 'we must rely not upon the people who wish to make the world safe for the British Empire, but upon those who don't.'

Within the cabinet, Brugha, Plunkett, and Markievicz all 'showed marked hostility' to the interview, but Griffith – with backing from Collins, deftly limited the discussion and secured acceptance of the President's explanation. The cabinet also authorised de Valera to spend the money he requested on the American elections.

As a result, the feud with Cohalan and Devoy erupted again at the Republican Party's National Convention in Chicago when de Valera deliberately undermined a Clan na Gael resolution calling for recognition of Ireland's right to self-determination. He contended Devoy and Cohalan were deliberately understating the Irish case by not asking for formal recognition of the Irish Republic.

This was clearly a bogus issue, seeing that de Valera had already accepted that the best political approach was to hammer away on the self-determination issue, because this was what the democracies were supposedly fighting for in the Great War. He not only endorsed this approach upon his arrival in the United States, but followed the same line in interviews with foreign correspondents upon his return to Ireland. In addition, he bitterly resented it when Seán T. O'Kelly adopted the position which he had taken himself at the Chicago convention. The dispute in the United States had nothing to do with principles, it was strictly a power struggle over who should speak for the Irish people and for the millions of Irish-Americans.

Devoy sought to drag Collins into the dispute by depicting him as the real Irish leader following his interview with Acker-mann. 'Michael Collins Speaks for Ireland', Devoy proclaimed boldly in a *Gaelic American* editorial. The weekly newspaper also carried a large front page photograph of Collins in uniform (taken in 1916), with the caption, 'Ireland's Fighting Chief'. There was no doubt Devoy was hitting at de Valera, but Collins wanted nothing to do with it.

'Every member of the Irish cabinet is in full accord with President de Valera's policy,' Collins wrote to Devoy on 30 September 1920. 'When he speaks to America, he speaks for all of us.'

These were not mere words. Collins actually went so far as to sever the IRB's connections with Clan na Gael a fortnight later. 'Let it be clearly understood,' he emphasised in a further letter to Devoy, 'that we all stand together, and that here at home every member of the cabinet has been an ardent supporter of the President against any and every group in America who have either not given him the co-operation which they should, or have set themselves definitely to thwart his actions.' Collins could not have been more forthright in his support of de Valera's position.

He clearly held de Valera in high esteem, and that affection was extended to the latter's family. Although the most wanted man in the country, Collins regularly visited de Valera's wife and children at their home in Greystones, County Wicklow. He brought Sineád money and news from America, and he also played with the children. Sineád de Valera sincerely appreciated his help. In later life she would go out of her way to tell members of the Collins family how much the visits had meant to her. She appreciated that he took the trouble to visit her personally, rather than sending messengers, as he could so easily have done.

In the summer of 1920 he arranged for her to visit the United States, but de Valera probably resented the gesture. He complained her place was at home with the children, and she promptly returned to Ireland. But there was a rather unseemly background to the visit, which had been prompted by ugly rumours about de Valera's relationship with his secretary, Kathleen O'Connell, whom he met in the United States. They had been travelling together, and it was rumoured they were having an affair.

De Valera actually planned to stay in the United States much longer, but he promptly cancelled those plans and returned to Ireland on hearing of Griffith's arrest. Probably even more disturbing was the news that Collins had taken over in Griffith's place. After all even Collins' friends had expressed reservations and helped block his selection as IRA Chief-of-Staff. Now he was in charge of the whole movement, and de Valera's alarm was understandable.

Upon his return de Valera lost no time in complaining about the way the IRA campaign was being conducted. 'Ye are going too fast,' he told Mulcahy on Christmas Eve. 'This odd shooting of a policeman here and there is having a very bad effect, from the propaganda point of view, on us in America. What we want is, one good battle about once a month with about 500 men on each side.'

Taking on the might of Britain in major battles was absurd in the eyes of Collins. If he had learned nothing else from the Easter Rebellion, he had learned that Ireland was militarily incapable of beating the British in an all-out fight. Thus he thought monthly battles with 500 men on each side would be sheer lunacy. It was obvious that de Valera was going to have problems in convincing him otherwise, so the President proposed that Collins should go to the United States.

Collins flatly rejected the idea, but de Valera pressed ahead and got cabinet approval of the scheme. He outlined the reasons in a long letter to Collins on 18 January 1921. With a new American President due to take office on 4 March, de Valera argued there would be a whole 'new political situation in the United States'. He wanted Collins to try to secure American support for Irish membership of the League of Nations in the event the United States joined the League. In putting forward a whole plethora of reasons for the proposed trip, de Valera seemed to be protesting a little too much. He stressed economic, financial, strategic, and propaganda benefits. He wanted Collins to try to heal the Irish-American split, and he made a naked appeal to Collins' vanity.

'You probably do not appreciate, as I do, what your presence will mean there for the cause, if only you will not be too modest to exploit your fame, or notoriety if you prefer it, but I would suggest that it be mainly on the lines of how moderate and full of commonsense you are,' de Valera wrote. As things stood there was a danger that the British could inflict a damaging blow if they managed to arrest the whole rebel leadership, but all the eggs would not be in one basket once Collins went to America. And, he argued, 'whatever coup the English may attempt, the line of succession is safe, and the future provided for.'

Despite all the protestations and flattery, Collins felt that de Valera was just trying to get him out of the way. He was indeed more moderate than was generally realised, but it was unlikely that anyone had ever before accused him of being overly modest.

'That long whore won't get rid of me as easy as that,' Collins remarked bitterly.

Maybe the proposal had something to do with Lloyd George's suggestion that Collins should leave Ireland for a while. De Valera certainly wanted to get negotiations going as quickly as possible. He actually wrote to Lloyd George in January suggesting secret talks. A successful visit to the United States by Collins would have the advantage of putting further pressure on the British government, which was already worried about the state of American opinion on the Irish question. Assistant Cabinet Secretary Tom Jones noted in his diary that the government were worried about 'the possibility of further compromising incidents' that might lead to 'the intervention of the United States'.

Thus de Valera was astutely interpreting the situation when he suggested the IRA's campaign should be waged in a way that could be best exploited in America for propaganda purposes. He began to take a leaf out of Lloyd George's book – making conciliatory sounds in public, while privately advocating a militant policy.

In an interview with a French journalist, for instance, de

Valera noted that the Allies had supposedly been fighting for the right of self-determination for all peoples in the recent war. 'If England should concede that right,' he said, 'there would be no further difficulties, either with her or with the Ulster minority. If Ulster should claim autonomy, we would be willing to grant it.' Asked if he would accept Dominion Status, he intimated such a settlement would be agreeable, seeing that even the leader of the British Conservative Party had publicly admitted that the Dominions had 'control of their whole destinies.'

'Thus,' de Valera emphasised, 'the British Dominions had conceded to them all the rights which the Irish Republicans demand. It is obvious that if these rights were not denied us, we would not be engaged in the present struggle.' He went on to stress that Sinn Féin was not a radical organisation at all. 'We are thoroughly sane and reasonable people, not a coterie of political doctrinaires, or even party politicians, Republican or other.'

His moderate statements were viewed with alarm in some Sinn Féin quarters, where people felt he should be calling for recognition of the Republican government. But he dismissed this.

'In public statements,' he maintained, 'our policy should be not to make it easy for Lloyd George by proclaiming that nothing but so and so will satisfy us. Our position should be simply that we are insisting on only one right, and that is the right of the people of this country to determine for themselves how they should be governed. That sounds moderate, but includes everything.' Yet this was the very issue on which he supposedly broke with Devoy and Cohalan.

It was widely interpreted that de Valera was offering to bargain on the extent of Irish freedom. As a propaganda ploy, it was certainly the impression he wished to give to the international press in order to force Britain to the conference table, but his efforts were being undermined by the unequivocal stand taken by Collins in his interview with Ackermann.

'Michael Collins is the soul of Ireland's fight for independence,' the Boston *American* declared. 'He has infinitely more sway in the country than President de Valera.'

The seeds of another power struggle – this time between de Valera and Collins – were already being sown. Both men wanted power, but there was a difference in their motives.

Collins sought power to achieve national goals, to get things done. To him the trappings of power – office and title – were not important. He had worked well under Griffith and Mulcahy while de Valera was in the United States. Mulcahy noted that Collins never crossed people who were working. He was quite content to work under Mulcahy, because he believed the Chief-of-Staff was doing the right thing.

De Valera, on the other hand, wanted power because it gave him status – something sadly lacking in his upbringing. Like Collins he had been reared in a tiny rural community in Munster, but their family circumstances were quite different. Collins had been reared as the youngest of a large, close-knit family in which he had not only been cherished but also spoiled. He grew up with an exaggerated sense of his own importance to become known as 'the Big Fellow', a facetious reflection of his own assumed importance. De Valera, on the other hand, could have had little inner conviction of his own value, because he was basically abandoned by his parents to be reared in loveless surroundings by his mother's family. Shortly after de Valera was born his father left the family and died two years later. The child was then sent to Ireland to be reared by his maternal grandmother, Elizabeth Coll.

Psychologists and psychiatrists have long recognised that the ultimate character of any individual is a result of an evolutionary process, with the early years of the child's life playing a vital part in shaping his, or her, future character. Thus, the earliest remembered childhood experiences provide a key to understanding the foundation on which the person's character develops.

Most adults cannot remember when they were only two years old, so when they do, those experiences are presumed to have had a particularly strong significançe. De Valera never forgot leaving New York, nor his first morning in Ireland when he woke up to find himself alone in his grandmother's house, fearing he had been abandoned completely. His mother visited him once in Bruree, just before she remarried in 1888. He pleaded with her to take him back, but she refused and continued to refuse even after she had started a second family. He was left in Bruree, where he went under the name of Eddie Coll, which fuelled speculation about his legitimacy. His mother had worked as a maid in the home of a local landowner before emigrating, and there were persistent rumours in the locality that she had left because she was pregnant and that young Eddie was the bastard son of the landlord's son.

De Valera's birth certificate would have demolished those

rumours because he was not born until some two years after his mother had emigrated, but he was in his thirties before anybody ever bothered to get a copy of that certificate. On winning a scholarship that allowed him to go to boarding school at the age of fifteen, he could not understand other boys being homesick; he was delighted with his deliverance from Bruree, and it was especially significant that he asked to be allowed to remain at the school for his first Christmas vacation, and he went to the home of a friend the following year. In later life, when de Valera had six children of his own, it was noteworthy that not one of them was named after anyone in his mother's family.

It was natural that an abandoned child should crave recognition. Spurred on subconsciously by his early rejection, he had a compulsion to become *somebody*, and when he achieved that recognition he had a driving need to hold it. As a child he looked in vain towards America for his mother to reclaim him. He must have thought that, if he had greater status, she would afford him that recognition which nearly everyone takes for granted. Within weeks of his election as *Priomh Aire* of the Dáil, he set out for the United States.

Collins could not understand why de Valera wanted to go to America, but de Valera probably did not understand it fully either. In addition to his rationale for the trip, there was his deep-rooted desire to demonstrate to his mother he was *somebody*. His title was therefore very important, and as most people in America would not understand the term *Priomh Aire*, he changed it to President.

Of course, it was not just a question of title alone. Without power, the title would have been meaningless. He was therefore determined to show he had more power than anybody else in the movement; he had to be clearly seen as the chief. This led to his problems with Cohalan and Devoy. In the same way it would also lead to a power struggle with Collins, which, in turn, would have disastrous consequences for the nation.

12. 'You'll Get None of My Men'

The year 1921 began badly for Collins when the home of Eileen McGrane at 21 Dawson Street was raided on New Year's Day. The British found a large cache of documents which she had been storing for him, among them were carbon copies of police reports typed by Broy.

This was another example of one of Collins' blind spots when it came to protecting his sources. Retaining those carbons was a costly piece of carelessness. If he needed the information, he should at least have had the documents transcribed because in their original form they quickly led to Broy's arrest. Collins tried to protect him by having a discreet warning issued to Detective Inspector McCabe, who was assigned to investigate Broy's activities. The inspector was told to go easy with his investigation if he valued his life. A similar warning was given to McCabe's boss, Chief Inspector Joe Supple. At the same time, Collins' people created a diversion by throwing suspicion on one of Broy's former colleagues, Pat McCarthy, a detective sergeant who had resigned from the DMP some months earlier under pressure from Collins.

McCarthy had been one of those who had tried to play both sides. He had his brother, a member of Sinn Féin, tell Collins he was not involved in political work but merely dealing with the licensing of taxis. On hearing this Collins produced a report, written by McCarthy, giving the names, addresses, and usual haunts of prominent Sinn Féiners.

'Ask him what has that to do with taxicabs?' Collins said, handing the document to the detective's brother.

That was enough for Detective Sergeant McCarthy; he promptly resigned from the force and emigrated to London. Now in order to take some of the heat off Broy, McCarthy was given a ticket to the United States, and his disappearance was made to look suspicious enough to raise doubts about Broy's guilt and thus save his life. Under the circumstances it was hardly surprising that Detective Inspector McCabe failed to come up with much of a case against Broy.

Meanwhile the search for Collins continued. Although de

Valera went into hiding following his return to Ireland, there was really no need as he was not wanted by the British. They could have arrested him virtually at will because they knew where he was living. But they could not find Collins despite frantic efforts.

Auxiliaries frequently burst into homes around the city shouting, 'Where's Michael Collins? We know he sleeps here!'

John Foley — a former secretary to the Lord Mayor of Dublin and well known for his antipathy to Sinn Féin — was arrested while having lunch with a former High Sheriff of Dublin, T. J. MacAvin in Jammet's restaurant on 10 January 1921.

'Come on Michael Collins, you've dodged us long enough,' the arresting officer said.

Despite their protestations, Foley and MacAvin were taken to Dublin Castle, before they could convince the officer of his mistake. Republicans were highly amused by the incident, which was all the funnier in that Foley did not look anything like Collins.

The following week some Crown authorities again thought they had Collins when they arrested a barman in the Prince of Wales Hotel using the name of Corry. He turned out to be a Michael Collins all right. 'But,' the *Irish Times* noted 'he is not the Michael Collins of IRA notoriety.'

The *Daily Sketch* reported that Collins had been shot off a white horse in trying to escape from Burgatia House on the outskirts of Roscarberry, County Cork, on 2 February. About thirty-five men had seized the house with the aim of attacking a nearby police barracks that night, but the Black and Tans learned of their presence and surrounded the premises with some one hundred men. The IRA force nevertheless managed to break out without suffering any casualties. One volunteer, Billy Sullivan, rode out on a bay mare which stumbled and fell, but he was uninjured. Needless to mention, Collins was not within a hundred miles of the place. He was amused when IRA intelligence intercepted a coded message asking for confirmation from Cork about the reported shooting. 'Is there any truth that Michael Collins was killed at Burgatia?' Dublin Castle asked.

'There is no information of the report *re* Michael Collins, but some believe he was wounded,' came the reply.

'We are hoping to hear further confirmation about poor Michael Collins,' the Big Fellow remarked facetiously in acknowledging the receipt of the two telegrams.

There was a further news agency report on 8 February that Collins had been killed in an engagement in Drimoleague, County Cork. Such reports added considerably to his notoriety, and for this, the British were largely responsible. Their frustrated forces sought to explain their failures by exaggerating the strength and the guile of their opponents, 'among whom,' Ormonde Winter (the Chief of British Intelligence) wrote, 'Michael Collins stands out pre-eminent.'

Following the Burgatia incident, the Black and Tans sought to excuse their failure by saying the IRA had a force of some five hundred men in the house, and the *Irish Times* credulously reported it. While those who took part must have known better, they seemed to attribute the amazing escape to the guile of Collins.

'He combined the characteristics of a Robin Hood with those of an elusive Pimpernel,' Winter explained. 'His many narrow escapes, when he managed to elude almost certain arrest, shrouded him in a cloak of historical romance'.

'The English papers have been giving me plenty of notoriety,' Collins wrote to his sister Lena on 5 March. 'The white horse story was an exaggeration.' It was not just an exaggeration, it was pure fiction. He was not next to near the place.

The *Daily Sketch* described Collins, according to himself, as a 'super hater, dour, hard, no ray of humour, [and] no trace of human feeling'. While the characterisation was wide of the mark, it probably did reflect Dublin Castle's distorted perception and thus explained the British difficulty in finding him. He was a very different type of person to the man they were looking for.

Certainly he could be serious and intent, but generally he had a breezy, affable manner. He went out of the way to be friendly with British troops or police. If he saw an area cordoned off he would go over and talk with those on guard duty. 'There are several of these fellows I don't know yet,' he would say to colleagues.

When stopped or searched himself, he would be cordial with the troops or Auxiliaries, would smile at them and joke with them. They naturally welcomed his friendliness in the hostile atmosphere permeating Ireland. 'You're a good sort anyway,' one of them said to him one day. He liked that; it appealed to his sense of humour. Such friendliness was the last thing the British expected of Michael Collins.

He liked to tell the story of talking to an Auxiliary in a Grafton

Street pub one day. 'That man Collins, I wish I could nail him,' Collins said.

'Don't worry,' replied the Auxiliary. 'His days are numbered.'

Collins related what happened with a roar of laughter and held up a calendar. 'See here,' he said to O'Reilly, 'how many days have I got to live?'

During early 1921 he had several narrow escapes of which the British were unaware, such as when the Auxiliaries raided 22 Mary Street, where he had his main finance office. They were primarily interested, however, in another office in the building. When he casually walked down the stairs, they merely searched him and then allowed him to leave the place.

One night he was staying at Susan Mason's house at 23 Brendan's Road when it was due to be raided, but the officer in charge of the raiding party mislaid his list in another house. In the course of a raid in Donnybrook, the officer had come across some love letters and was reading them when the woman to whom they had been sent entered the room and upbraided him for his ungentlemanly conduct. The embarrassed officer hurriedly stuffed the letters back into a drawer and inadvertently included his own list of houses to be raided that night. She found the list and passed it on to Batt O'Connor next day, when Collins then learned of his narrow escape.

He had another close call in Kirwin's Bar one night when it was raided. He was with Sergeant Maurice McCarthy of the RIC who had just come down from Belfast with the latest police codes. Everyone in the bar was being searched but when McCarthy produced his RIC identification, the officer in charge invited him and Collins to have a drink. Had they searched Collins they would have found the codes.

It was widely believed there was a reward of £10,000 for the capture of Collins, which was as much as most Irish people could then expect to earn in a lifetime. The Black and Tans, for instance, were considered well paid, but the supposed reward amounted to more than they could earn in fifty years, working seven days a week and fifty-two weeks a year. As a result there was always the danger someone might betray Collins for the money. The British arrested Christy Harte and offered him his freedom and a sizeable reward if he would telephone a certain number the next time Collins visited Vaughan's Hotel. Harte agreed, but promptly told Collins about the promise which he had no intention of keeping.

William Doran, the porter at the Wicklow Hotel, however, was apparently a different case. He was suspected of betraying some people, and Collins ordered the Squad to shoot him. Joe Dolan took a taxi to the hotel on 30 January. He arrived with two heavy suitcases for Doran to carry. And as the porter was laden down, Dolan shot him dead in the hotel. Doran had assisted Collins in the past and his widow thought he had been killed by British agents. She therefore appealed to the Sinn Féin regime for funds as she had three small children. Collins ordered she be given the money and, for her children's sake, not be told the true circumstances leading to her husband's death.

'The poor little devils need the money,' he said..

It was a humane response towards the family of a man whose death he had ordered, but he did not have the authority for such a gesture. It was the kind of thing which raised questions about his handling of finances.

Brugha needled Collins relentlessly to provide the cabinet with a proper accounting of money allocated to purchase arms in Scotland. There was a discrepancy which Collins was unable to resolve. In the light of the pressure under which he was operating, together with the amount of money he had handled, the discrepancy was of no significance, other than as a whipping horse to attack his administrative credibility, if not his actual integrity. Things got so bad that Mulcahy complained to de Valera about Brugha's attitude towards Collins.

'You know,' de Valera told him, 'I think Cathal is jealous of Mick. Isn't it a terrible thing to think that a man with the qualities that Cathal undoubtedly has would fall a victim to a dirty little vice like jealousy.'

A small, sincere, resolute man, Brugha was dedicated to the cause with the zeal of a fanatic. While he and others worked unselfishly, seeking no glory for themselves, he resented all the press attention given to Collins. Much as Mulcahy disliked Brugha's attitude, he never doubted his sincerity. 'He was naturally blunt and frank and was no more intending to intrigue than he was to diplomacy,' Mulcahy noted.

A selfless, unassuming patriot, Brugha resented Collins for seeking personal glory and presuming too much.

The Big Fellow was not content with his own legitimate ambit; he was always ready to take anything upon himself which he thought was for the good of the movement, even if it meant meddling in the affairs of ministerial colleagues.

With his well organised intelligence network, he was particularly well-placed to interfere. He knew more about what was happening throughout the movement than anyone, and he was able to exert considerable influence through an IRB clique of fellow-Corkmen in key administrative positions. For instance, he managed to have himself replaced as Adjutant General of the IRA by Gearóid O'Sullivan, and as Director of Organisation by Diarmuid O'Hegarty, who also became secretary to the government. Seán Ó Muirthile replaced Collins as Secretary of the Supreme Council of the IRB, and Pádraig O'Keeffe was elected Joint National Secretary of Sinn Féin. Collins' influence with them was based largely on their recognition of his enormous organisational talents.

'A vast amount of stuff could be assembled associating his smiling buoyancy, his capacity for bearing tension, clearness of mind, perfectly controlled calm, and a devil-may-carishness,' wrote Mulcahy. 'His clarity of mind and his whole manner and demeanour, together with his power of concentration on the immediate matter in hand, gave him a great power over men.'

Brugha so loathed the Big Fellow's personality, however, that he was apparently unable to see, much less appreciate, those qualities which so many admired. He mistakenly believed Collins used his IRB position to acquire his influence, whereas, in fact, he acquired the position because he already had the influence as a result of his administrative ability.

Maybe Collins' interference would have been more acceptable if he had not resented similar interference in his own areas. He seemed to think others should abide by certain rules, while he should be able to improvise as he went along.

'What the hell do you know about finance?' he snapped at Stack one day when the latter had the temerity to make some suggestion.

Like a typical Kerryman, Stack responded with a question of his own: 'And what the hell do you know about manners, Mick?'

Though Collins and Brugha both belonged to the militant wing of the movement, there was a difference in their militancy. Brugha was rather dull-witted, or as de Valera put it, 'a bit slow'. He basically reacted to events, whereas Collins provoked them. For instance, Brugha had disapproved of the Soloheadbeg ambush which marked the beginning of the War of Independence, while Collins warmly approved of it and encouraged similar attacks throughout the country in the hope of provoking the

Crown forces to react with a ferocity which would drive the Irish people into the hands of the IRA. This was the colossal mistake which the British had made in the aftermath of the Easter Rebellion, and they would make it again in the form of the Black and Tan terror.

Collins had deliberately provoked the Black and Tan War in order to secure the support of the Irish people, but in the process he unleashed forces which he could not control and which would ultimately bring about his own death. Infuriated by the savagery of Crown forces, Brugha wanted to resurrect his old scheme to kill members of the British cabinet. Collins had been involved in the earlier move; he had sent Tobin to London to investigate the possibility of killing cabinet members, but the scheme was abandoned when Tobin concluded the attack would be suicidal as the only feasible place for it was Downing Street. Later, when Brugha sought to revive the scheme Collins realised this would be to make the same kind of mistake as the British had made in Ireland – killing cabinet members would drive the British people into the arms of their militants. Hence he resolutely opposed Brugha's proposal.

'You'll get none of my men for that,' he declared.

'That's all right, Mr Collins, I want none of *your* men. I'll get my own.'

Brugha called Seán MacEoin to Dublin and outlined the scheme to him. MacEoin agreed somewhat reluctantly to lead the attack.

'This is madness,' Collins thundered when MacEoin told him about the plan. 'Do you think that England has the makings of only one cabinet?' He suggested MacEoin consult the Chief-of-Staff.

'I was appalled at the idea,' Mulcahy recalled. He 'upbraided MacEoin' for coming to Dublin, and ordered him to go back to his command area and have nothing further to do with the proposed London project. On his way back by train, MacEoin was recognised and ran into a whole party of Auxiliaries at the railway station in Longford. He was arrested and was shot and seriously wounded when he tried to escape. His capture was a serious blow because he was one of the best IRA commanders and probably the most effective outside the Cork area.

'It is simply disastrous,' Collins wrote. 'Cork will be fighting alone now.'

Collins, who wrote that he 'would almost prefer that the

worst would have happened' than that MacEoin should have fallen into the hands of the enemy, immediately set about planning an escape as it was obvious the British would execute MacEoin as soon as he was fit enough to be tried and hanged.

While escape plans were being formulated, Collins' intelligence operations suffered a devastating reversal with the discovery of his office at 5 Mespil Road, where most of his documents were stored. He had just left for the evening on 1 April, when the building was raided by the British. They were obviously acting on a tip. They found a considerable volume of material and staked out the office for his return next day. Patricia Hoey and her mother, who lived in the house were held captive.

As they waited through the night Hoey came up with a scheme to warn Collins. She got her mother to pretend to become seriously ill and persuaded the British to allow her to summon a doctor. Alice Barry, the doctor who had put up Breen at her home while he was recuperating some months earlier, was summoned and told of the trap set for Collins. She managed to get word to Joe O'Reilly, and Collins and his staff were intercepted and warned next morning.

'They waited for me all day Saturday,' Collins wrote to de Valera, 'the lady says they were so frightened they certainly would not have hit me in any case.'

It was a touch of that raw vanity, which some people found obnoxious. The British had little to fear from Collins himself, as far as Brugha was concerned, because there was no evidence he ever fired a shot at any of them. While Collins had been in the GPO during Easter Week 1916, he would have had very little opportunity to fire at anyone then because Crown forces had given the building a wide berth and had merely shelled it from afar. In view of the regularity with which people were stopped and searched in the streets of Dublin during the ensuing War of Independence, Collins did not normally carry any weapons, which really required a considerable amount of courage, especially when one considers the fate of his friends Dick McKee and Peadar Clancy.

Men like Tom Barry and Liam Deasy, who visited Dublin during the early spring, marvelled at the fearless way in which Collins moved about the city. Although they had both come up from the thick of the fighting in West Cork, they found Dublin unnerving. Deasy and Gearóid O'Sullivan's brother, Tadgh, met Collins in Devlin's bar and soon found themselves at a race-meeting in Phoenix Park, with the place crawling with military and police. Yet Collins and his people showed no fear. 'Nothing would do him now but to bring us into the reserved stand where we stood shoulder to shoulder with the enemy,' Deasy noted.

'Good God!' Tadgh O'Sullivan exclaimed, 'these fellows are mad.'

'They seemed to have no fear of arrest, or if they had, they did not show it,' Barry wrote. 'Their lack of precautions was amazing and even made one angry.'

'One night at about nine o'clock,' Barry recalled, 'we ran into a hold-up by about fifty Auxiliaries.' They were each searched. 'I was next to Collins and he put up such a fine act, joking and blasting in turn, that he had the whole search party of terrorists in good humour in a short time.' Needless to say they were not detained, but Barry was critical that Collins had not taken the precaution of sending a scout ahead.

'Mick as usual guffawed and chaffed me about being a windy West Cork beggar,' Barry noted. 'Failing to see the joke, I told him crossly that it was quite true, I was a windy beggar, as I had a wholesome regard for my neck.'

For months de Valera had been emphasising the Irish side was prepared to negotiate a settlement with the British, but Collins adopted a quite different line when he gave another interview to Carl Ackermann in early April. He told the American correspondent the IRA was going to continue the fight 'until we win'.

'What are your terms of settlement?' Ackermann asked.

'Lloyd George has a chance of showing himself to be a great statesman by recognising the Irish Republic.'

'Do you mean a Republic within the British Commonwealth of Nations or outside?'

'No, I mean an Irish Republic.'

'Why are you so hopeful?'

'Because I know the strength of our forces and I know our position is infinitely stronger throughout the world,' Collins explained. 'The terror the British wanted to instil in this country has completely broken down. It is only a question of time until we shall have them cleared out.'

'So you are still opposed to compromise?'

'When I saw you before I told you that the same effort which would get us Dominion Home Rule would get us a Republic. I am still of that opinion, and we have never had so many peace moves as we have had since last autumn.'

The British actually concluded there was a power struggle going on within the Sinn Féin movement in which de Valera was little more than a figurehead, crying in the wilderness for a negotiated settlement, while Collins, the real leader, wanted to fight it out to the bitter end.

'De Valera and Michael Collins have quarrelled,' Lloyd George told his cabinet on 27 April. 'The latter will have a Republic and he carries a gun and he makes it impossible to negotiate. De Valera cannot come here and say he is willing to give up Irish Independence, for if he did, he might be shot.'

Dublin Castle had been predicting the IRA was on the verge of collapse before Christmas, but by April this collapse seemed no nearer.

'The tenacity of the IRA is extraordinary,' Tom Jones wrote to Bonar Law. 'Where was Michael Collins during the Great War? He would have been worth a dozen brass hats.'

While Collins' bold statements undoubtedly contributed to the impression that the IRA was full of fight, and in turn undermined the credibility of Dublin Castle, they also undermined de Valera's efforts to force the British to the conference table. The President later told his authorised biographers that from April 1921 'Collins did not accept my view of things as he had done before and was inclined to give public expression to his own opinions even when they differed from mine.'

De Valera and Brugha moved to whittle away at Collins' power base. The Squad was amalgamated with the Dublin Brigade, and Collins was replaced by Stack as the designated substitute in the event anything happened to the President.

Lloyd George wanted to negotiate but he felt it would be pointless talking with de Valera because Collins was the real leader, and he was afraid of the political repercussions among Conservatives if he talked with Collins.

'The question is whether I can see Michael Collins,' he said. 'No doubt he is the head and front of the movement. If I could see him, a settlement might be possible. The question is whether the British people would be willing for us to negotiate with the head of a band of murderers.'

When the British cabinet discussed the possibility of a truce on 12 May, the Prime Minister remarked that 'de Valera does not agree with the gun business' but he was being spied upon by Collins, who was depicted as being 'against compromise.' Churchill, who had been one of the most vocal proponents of the

British terror, was now showing distinct signs of wavering.

'We are getting an odious reputation,' he declared, adding that it was 'poisoning' Britain's relations with the United States. He was therefore in favour of a truce.

But there was no point in having a truce without trying to negotiate a settlement, and Austen Chamberlain, the newly elected leader of the Conservative Party, saw no point in this 'as long as de Valera is at the mercy of Michael Collins.'

'You can't make a truce without meeting with Michael Collins,' Lord Fitz Alan declared. 'We can't have that.'

The cabinet divided, with Churchill and four other Liberal Party ministers in favour of a truce, while Lloyd George sided with the Conservative majority. But a fortnight later the British had to reconsider the Irish situation in the light of further developments. On 24 May Brigadier General Frank Crozier, the recently resigned head of the Auxiliaries, went public with a blistering attack on the conduct of some of his own men and the Black and Tans. He admitted they had fired into the crowd in Croke Park on Bloody Sunday without provocation. Maybe the pressure on the British government would not have been as great, if the Crown forces were being seen to be making progress, but the reverse was evident. Next day the IRA attacked the Custom House in Dublin in what was the Irish side's largest single operation since the Easter Rebellion. As a result the casualty figures of the Crown forces soared. The seventy-two police and soldiers killed that month made a mockery of Greenwood's repeated predictions that the IRA was about to collapse.

The IRA in Dublin was virtually decimated with the killing of five members and the capture of some eighty more. On Thursday, 26 May, Crown forces raided Collins' office at 22 Mary Street just after lunch and narrowly missed him. He had transferred his intelligence office there following the raid on Mespil Road and would normally have been there at the time, but had a foreboding during lunch with Gearóid O'Sullivan and decided not to return to the office that afternoon.

'I ought to have been there at that precise moment,' Collins wrote a few days later. 'They depended too much on my punctuality.' But Bob Conlon, his messenger boy was arrested and taken to Dublin Castle.

'They did not ill-treat him,' Collins explained with characteristic vanity, because they 'thought if they did that M.C. would murder them all.' In fact, however, they did mistreat the boy, by using thumb screws on him. And Collins found himself just one step ahead of the Crown forces in the following days.

'I may tell you the escape of Thursday was nothing to four or five escapes I have had since,' he wrote to de Valera on 1 June. 'They ran me very close for quite a good while on Sunday evening.' He still tried to think of himself not being *on the run.*

'He is on the run who feels he is on the run,' Collins wrote Moya Llewelyn Davies in June. 'I have avoided that feeling.'

Although the IRA had suffered devastating losses in Dublin as a result of the attack on the Four Courts, the venture turned up trumps on the propaganda front. With all the publicity the British government was forced to change its policy. At first it was decided to declare martial law throughout the twenty-six counties and intensify their campaign. Collins learned through his sources that British forces were going to be trebled, and would intensify their operations, especially their searches and internment. 'All means of transport, from push bicycles up, will be commandeered, and allowed only on permit,' he warned de Valera.

Before implementing such a policy, however, Lloyd George was advised to make a genuine effort to negotiate a settlement. Otherwise, Jan Christian Smuts, the South African Premier, predicted irreparable damage would be done to relations within the British Commonwealth. Smuts played a role in persuading the British to propose talks. It was decided to use the occasion of the opening of the new Northern Ireland Parliament by King George V on 22 June to foreshadow the more conciliatory approach.

This process was nearly upscuttled the same day when de Valera was arrested by British soldiers who apparently did not realise their government had ordered he should be left alone. He was released next morning, however, and asked to make himself available for a communication from the British government. This led to the signing of a Truce on 11 July, and de Valera went over to London the following day for talks with Lloyd George.

The Anglo-Irish War was over, but Collins clearly visualised darker clouds gathering on the political horizon. 'At this moment,' he wrote on 13 July, 'there is more ill-will within a victorious assembly than ever could be anywhere else except in the devil's assembly. It cannot be fought against. The issues and persons, are mixed to such an extent as to make discernibility an utter impossibility except for a few.'

De Valera had set out for London with a large delegation. Collins wanted to go with him, but the President flatly refused to have him, and there were some heated words between them. Collins was obviously despondent afterwards. 'This is a time when jealousy and personal gain count for more than country,' he wrote ominously.

Epilogue

Eventually a bitter feud would develop between de Valera and Collins. Although both would profess a personal affection and deep trust of each other in the coming months, neither was telling the truth. They already distrusted one another deeply during the final months of the war.

Throughout the struggle they were often at cross purposes. Their first major difference, which occurred before they had even met, was over the selection of the rebel prisoner, Joe McGuinness, to stand for parliament in the Longford by-election of 1917. Contending that a defeat at the polls would set back the separatist cause, de Valera persuaded McGuinness to decline the nomination, but Collins ignored the instruction by having him nominated anyway, and the gamble paid off. McGuinness was elected, if only by a very narrow margin.

In those early days de Valera portrayed himself as a soldier with little time for politics – sentiments which Collins heartily shared, so the latter became an ardent supporter when the former moved to unite the various separatist groups under the Sinn Féin banner later that year. In his first presidential address to the party, de Valera talked about waiting for the proper moment to 'draw the naked sword' in order to force the British to do likewise.

To prepare for that moment Collins, as Director of Organisation, set about building the IRA into a disciplined, well-organised force. It was he who put together the movement's brilliant intelligence system. With the experiences gained while interned at Frongoch, he organised a communications' network with those in prison and then established a group to arrange jail breaks. In February 1919 he master-minded de Valera's escape from Lincoln Jail in the belief that the time had come to 'draw the naked sword', but de Valera had other ideas; he now advocated that the political route offered the best hope of success. He was not only unwilling to take up the sword but moved to prevent anyone else doing so by re-organising the Sinn Féin Executive so that the more politically-minded were strengthened at the expense of militants like Collins, whose unpredictability frightened even some of his own closest colleagues.

Collins played a vital role, as Minister for Finance, in collecting the money which was used to finance the movement's activities at home. He was a demanding task-master, always pushing and driving to get things done. He pushed everyone, especially himself. Although de Valera subsequently collected much more money in the United States, very little of it ever got back to Ireland. Hence Collins deserved the credit for organising the funding, but his greatest contribution was in the area of intelligence. Here he relied on the assistance of a tremendous number of people from all walks of life, and he had the uncanny ability of being on intimate terms with most of them while at the same time somehow managing to remain invisible to the British authorities. Throughout the movement people looked to him for action.

Anybody who wanted anything done was told to see Collins. With his well-organised intelligence network, he knew what was happening throughout the movement, and he was able to exert considerable influence through an IRB clique of fellow-Corkmen in key administrative positions. His influence with them, however, was based mainly on their recognition of his enormous organisational talents, and not any special authority as President of the IRB.

Some critics charged Collins with interfering in the affairs of colleagues, but Mulcahy, who was in a particularly good position to judge, noted that 'Collins never crossed the bows of anybody who was doing work and particularly anybody in authority.' He obviously worked well with Griffith, seeing that the latter wanted him as his successor as acting President. In addition, Collins could not have been more forthright in his support of the President against Devoy and Cohalan, despite some reservations about the way things were being handled in the United States. Later, however, in the final months of the war he certainly did cross de Valera.

Collins was a complex personality in which good and bad were so intertwined as to make an objective assessment exceptionally difficult. His able, restless, ambitious temperament was never content within its own legitimate ambit. He was like a torrent constantly overflowing too constricted banks. He could be a warm, friendly, passionate, boisterous, fun-loving and generous individual with a moderate and rational outlook, and he could just as easily be a cold, dour, unreasonable and utterly ruthless person – an arrogant bully with a ferocious temper and a mean vindictive streak. There is no evidence he ever killed anybody himself, but he was not afraid to order the deaths of people standing in his way. He was even prepared to take hostages to further his aims. At one point in 1919 he advocated kidnapping the American President, Woodrow Wilson, then visiting London while on his way to the Paris Peace Conference. Even some of those closest to Collins were afraid that his fanatical determination knew no prudent bounds, and hence they passed over him to select Richard Mulcahy as IRA Chief-of-Staff.

It was while de Valera was in the United States that Collins gradually managed to implement a bold, calculated policy which was designed not only to destroy Britain's intelligence-gathering apparatus but, even more importantly, to undermine her administration in Ireland. In the latter half of 1919 and 1920 Collins steadily expanded his influence, using violence and terrorism as his main weapons. He deliberately provoked the Crown authorities into over-reacting in such a way as to alienate the overwhelming majority of the Irish people.

Collins was the prototype of the modern urban terrorist and indeed the architect of the Black and Tan War. He organised his Squad in June 1919 with the immediate aim of systematically killing selected policemen. The most efficient detectives in G Division of the DMP were ruthlessly cut down. Smith, Hoey, Wharton, Barton, and Redmond were all shot under orders from Collins. And he was not content with eliminating effective policemen, he also sought to strike at the personal symbol of the British connection by trying to assassinate Sir John French, the Lord Lieutenant.

In 1916 the British had over-reacted following the Easter Rebellion – not only by executing the leaders but also in rounding up thousands of people who had nothing to do with the rising – and Collins astutely anticipated that they would over-react again. They launched what the British Cabinet Secretary, Sir Maurice Hankey, described as a 'counter-murder' campaign in which reprisals would become the order of the day in Ireland.

Deprived of proper intelligence, the British forces struck out blindly at the nationalist population, burning houses, and 'shooting up' towns and villages. They made the mistake of considering all nationalists their enemies. Although most Irish people outside the north-east were nationalists, this did not mean they supported the IRA. For example, the number of nationalists who volunteered for the Crown forces during the First World War was many times greater than that which served with the IRA during the War of Independence. But when the British lashed out blindly against all nationalists, when they took out innocent people and shot them as reprisals, they totally alienated the overwhelming majority of Irish people and won for Collins and the IRA a degree of support which they would probably never have gained otherwise.

The British forces were given virtual *carte blanche* to kill anyone suspicious, and they were authorised to infiltrate undercover agents who were charged with the task of eliminating what were described as 'would-be assassins'. The excesses of the British campaign were not just the product of some over-zealous commanders in emotional settings; the policy of 'counter-murder' had the backing of the British government at the highest level, with the approval and support of people like Prime Minister David Lloyd George and his Minister for War, Winston Churchill, that supposed paragon of twentieth century democracy and freedom. Churchill clamoured for executions in Ireland. Although a vocal opponent of the Russian Revolution, he advocated in cabinet that Britain should imitate the Bolsheviks by sending some specially selected judges around Ireland without delay to dispense 'summary justice'. Field Marshal Sir Henry Wilson, the Chief of Imperial General Staff wanted to take the counter-murder policy a step further. He advocated drawing up, and displaying publicly on church doors, formal rosters with the names of people to be executed in retaliation for the killing of any members of the Crown forces. Such a scheme would have required the political leaders to take formal responsibility for the policy of 'counter-murder', which, of course, they were not prepared to do openly.

Collins quickly learned about the sinister British scheme from his own agents, who managed to identify many of the culprits. 'Inspector Swanzy and his associates put Lord Mayor MacCurtain away, so I got Swanzy and all his associates wiped out, one by one, in all parts of Ireland to which they had been secretly dispersed,' Collins explained afterwards. 'I found out that these fellows we put on the spot were going to put a lot of us on the spot, so I got in first.'

He would have had people believe that it was the British who had started 'the vicious circle' of assassination, or 'the murder race' as he called it. When asked about the killings of policemen in 1918 and 1919, he dismissed those as 'spasmodic' incidents 'for arms and the like – not inspired by a central authority'. That was probably true of the killings of 1918 and early 1919. The ambush at Soloheadbeg, where the two policemen were killed in January 1919 – which is generally regarded as the start of the War of Independence – was strictly a local incident. Collins was not involved, but he was behind the killings of the various detectives from G Division of the DMP in the latter half of 1919 before the British ever introduced the so-called Cairo Gang. Even though Collins claimed he was playing the British 'at their own game', it was he, in fact, who had started the centrally organised killings in 1919, and the British then made the mistake of trying to play him at his game, but their sources of intelligence were never a match for his. He was always able to stay one step ahead of them.

In November 1920 Lloyd George was openly proclaiming that he had 'murder by the throat', as his agents were closing in on Collins and his men. Just how close they were became evident in the early hours of Bloody Sunday, 21 November, when they arrested two of his closest associates – Dick McKee and Peadar Clancy – just hours before the two of them were due to take part in operations designed to wipe out the British undercover network. Eleven or twelve of the undercover agents were killed in the subsequent operations, and the British then reacted with the callous stupidity that was symptomatic of so much of their conduct at this stage of the conflict. They raided a football match in Dublin and fired indiscriminately into the crowd, killing more than a dozen totally innocent people, including one of the players on the field.

In the aftermath of Bloody Sunday, Griffith was arrested and Collins took over as acting President. He held the office for four hectic weeks, amid the Clune negotiations, some of the bloodiest fighting, the most widespread round up of suspects since the Easter Rebellion, and the transfer of the campaign to Britain for the first time. He was unquestionably the most wanted man in Ireland.

It was widely believed there was a reward on his head of £10,000, then a veritable fortune. While no such reward was ever offered for his actual capture, that kind of money was available for information leading to the conviction of those behind the attempt on the life of the Lord Lieutenant or any of the killings of the G Division detectives. Collins had been behind all those events, so some of his colleagues could have made considerably more than £10,000 by betraying him, though it was unlikely any such traitor would have lived to enjoy the money for very long.

De Valera had planned to stay in the United States much longer, but he promptly cancelled his plans and returned to Ireland following Griffith's arrest. The news that Collins had taken over probably sparked his return. After all even Collins' friends had expressed reservations and helped block his selection as IRA Chief-of-Staff. Now he was in charge of the whole movement, and de Valera's hasty return was understandable.

Having been safe in the United States throughout the terror while Collins was being hunted in Ireland, however, it was insensitive of the President to criticise the way the campaign had been run without, at least, waiting for a few days and talking to some people before he advocated a drastic change in policy. His actions certainly implied criticism of Collins, and the latter's feelings could hardly have been reassured when, with indecent haste, the President tried to send him to the United States.

Collins refused to go, but de Valera pressed ahead and got cabinet approval for the scheme. It seemed to Collins that an effort was being made to get him out of the way. And he was probably right in his assessment. The whole affair certainly did not foster trust.

The seeds of the coming power struggle between de Valera and Collins were being sown. Both men wanted power, but there was a difference in their motives.

Collins sought power to achieve national goals, to get things done. To him the trappings of power – office and title – were not important. As the youngest child in a large, close-knit family, he felt wanted and he grew up sure of himself; whereas there was no such security in de Valera's background. He had been virtually abandoned by his mother and grew up with a deep-seated craving to be somebody. He needed power and position. And now that he had those, he was deeply suspicious, indeed almost paranoid, of anybody who might take them away from him. As he said himself, he had hardly arrived in the United States when he realised the country was not big enough for himself and Cohalan, and he was hardly back in Ireland when he seemed to think there was no room for Collins.

Mulcahy felt de Valera was jealous because Collins had become the popular hero of the struggle. News reports contributed greatly to Collins' notoriety, and the British were largely responsible for this because they attributed their failure, not to their own failings, but to his genius. They grossly exaggerated his strength and guile, and in the process he became a charismatic figure enveloped in a cloak of historical romance.

This annoyed Brugha, who resented the publicity giving Collins credit for running the whole campaign. He was further irritated in mid-May when the New York *American* carried an interview with Collins, whom it described as 'Commander-in Chief' of the Irish forces, even though – as Director of Intelligence – he was basically only a section head. While Collins was hardly responsible for the exaggerated publicity, he made no effort to rectify the situation, so he effectively took credit which belonged to others, at least that was how Brugha saw it. The latter grew to despise Collins and was particularly resentful at his interference in a scheme to kill members of the British cabinet. Collins, who thought the planned move would be politically disastrous, did intervene but only after he had been approached by MacEoin. He did not tell MacEoin to abandon the scheme; he just suggested he consult the Chief-of-Staff, who promptly called the whole thing off.

De Valera also resented interference in the following weeks when he sought to take political and military initiatives by publicly advocating negotiations and privately suggesting the IRA take on the British in major battles involving up to 500 men each month. He wanted the military campaign waged so that it could be best exploited in America for propaganda purposes. Here he astutely assessed the situation, because the British were so worried about American opinion at the time that even Churchill, who had been one of the most outspoken advocates of repression, was coming round to the idea of negotiations. Collins, however, had strong reservations about de Valera's call for major battles. The Easter Rebellion had demonstrated that Ireland did not have the military capability of beating the British in an all out fight. Hence he thought the proposal was absurd, and he ridiculed it within the ranks of the IRA. In addition, he publicly emphasised the IRA's determination to carry the fight to a successful conclusion.

His bold public statements refuted Dublin Castle's contention that the IRA was virtually beaten and thus may well have contributed to the British government's eventual decision to negotiate, but the statements were unhelpful from de Valera's standpoint because they tended to undermine his efforts to force the British to the conference table. The British concluded there was a power struggle within Sinn Féin in which Collins was the real leader and the President little more than a figurehead, and hence they thought it would be pointless talking to de Valera.

There was indeed a power struggle, but Collins was coming off worst. De Valera and Brugha had been moving to whittle away at his power base. The Squad was amalgamated with the Dublin Brigade, and Collins himself was replaced by Stack as the designated minister to take over in the event anything happened to the President.

De Valera also got his way on the issue of a major battle when the IRA attacked the Custom House in late May. It was the Irish side's largest single operation since the Easter Rebellion. While it was a military disaster, it was an unqualified success from the propaganda standpoint because it finally convinced the British government that its current campaign was a failure. Faced with this realisation, Lloyd George and his colleagues soon decided to seek a negotiated settlement, and they agreed to a truce. The war was over.

No one man ever won a war, and it was hardly accurate to say that the Irish side won this war, seeing that few if any Irish nationalists saw Ireland as less than the whole island. One consequence of the war was the partitioning of the island, which was certainly not something for which the Irish side was fighting. Characterising Collins therefore as 'the man who won the war' was really a piece of hyperbole.

Yet he did arguably make the biggest individual contribution towards whatever was won. He was probably the man most responsible for starting the war, and in the last analysis he also played the main Irish role in the peace negotiations leading to the Anglo-Irish Treaty, which he signed in the full realisation that he was signing his own death warrant. At the time he thought he had secured the means of ending partition and achieving the full national goal, but his part in those negotiations is a different story which is told elsewhere.

Notes

The sources for all quoted material are given in these notes. The reference numbers refer to pages and paragraphs ending on the various pages. Thus 101/1 refers to material quoted in the first paragraph ending on page 101. In this specific instance the quoted material actually appears in the unfinished paragraph at the end of page 100.

Chapter 1 (pp. 7-17)
7/1 Dáil Éireann, *Official Report: Debate on the Treaty Between Great Britain and Ireland*, 20.
7/2 *Ibid.*, 327.
7/4 *Ibid.*, 325.
8/4 Hayden Talbot, *Michael Collins' Own Story as told to Hayden Talbot*, 23.
8/7-8 *Ibid.*
9/1 Collins to Kevin O'Brien, 16 October 1916.
9/3-4 Rex Taylor, *Michael Collins*, 26-7.
10/1 Talbot, *Michael Collins' Own Story*, 25.
10/2-3 Frank O'Connor, *The Big Fellow: Michael Collins and the Irish Revolution*, 20.
11/4-5 Minutes of AGM of Geraldine Club, Ms. NLI.
12/2-3 Michael Collins, *The Path to Freedom*, 122-3.
12/5 Taylor, *Michael Collins*, 33.
12/6 Piaras Beaslaí, *Michael Collins and the Making of the New Ireland*, 1:80.
13/1 *Ibid.*
13/4 *Ibid.*, 1:304.
14/4 Taylor, *Michael Collins*, 31.
15/1 Collins to Seán Deasy, 5 January 1916.
15/2 Colm Connolly, 'The Shadow of Béal na mBláth,' RTE, TV, 1989.
16/4 Christopher Andrew, *Secret Service: The Making of the British Intelligence Community*, 356.

Chapter 2 (pp. 18-28)
18/4 Thomas M. Coffey, *Agony at Easter: The 1916 Rising*, 4.
18/7 Ruth Dudley Edwards, *Patrick Pearse: The Triumph of Failure*, 277.
18/9 Caulfield, *The Easter Rebellion*, 22.
19/3-4 *Ibid.*, 25.
19/5 *Ibid.*, 27.
19/7 Proclamation of Irish Republic.
20/1 Coffey, *Agony at Easter*, 75.
20/3 *Ibid.*, 39.
20/5-6 Dudley Edwards, *Patrick Pearse*, 291.
21/3-4 Coffey, *Agony at Easter*, 157.
21/5 Desmond FitzGerald *Memoirs of Desmond FitzGerald, 1913-16*, 144.
21/7 *Ibid.*
22/1-3 Peadar Kerney, 'The Soldier's Song'.
22/4 Coffey, *Agony at Easter*, 154.
23/1 Pearse's address, 27 April, 1916, q. Coffey, *Agony at Easter*, 171-2.
23/2-3 Patrick Pearse, *The Political Writings and Speeches of Patrick Pearse*, Desmond Ryan, ed., 299.
23/4 see Xavier Carty, *In Bloody Protest: The Tragedy of Patrick Pearse*, 51-66.
24/1-2 Pádraic Pearse, 'Little Lad of the Tricks,' *Plays, Stories, Poems*, 316.
24/3 Coffey, *Agony at Easter*, 76.

24/4 Collins to Kevin O'Brien, 6 October 1916.
24/5 Dudley Edwards, *Patrick Pearse*, 245.
24/6 Collins to Kevin O'Brien, 6 October, 1916.
25/1 *Ibid.*; and 9 November, 1916.
25/3 Collins to Kevin O'Brien, 6 October 1916.
25/5 Dudley Edwards, *Patrick Pearse*, 299.
26/2 Caulfield, *Easter Rebellion*, 320.
26/6-10 Coffey, *Agony at Easter*, 254-5.
27/1 *Ibid.*, 255.
27/5-6 Desmond Ryan, *Remembering Sion*, 207.
27/8-9 Coffey, *Agony at Easter*, 260.
27/10 Ryan, *Remembering Sion*, 208.
28/3-4 Ulick O'Connor, A *Terrible Beauty*, 116.

Chapter 3 (pp. 29-39)
29/3 Joe Sweeney, interview, Kenneth Griffith and Timothy E. O'Grady, *Curious Journey: An Oral History of Ireland's Unfinished Revolution*, 93.
29/6-8 Ryan, *Remembering Sion*, 211.
30/1 Collins to Hannie Collins, 16 May 1916.
30/2 Sweeney interview, *Curious Journey*, 93.
30/3-4 Ryan, *Remembering Sion*, 215.
30/5 Margery Forester, *Michael Collins: The Lost Leader*, 52.
30/6-7 Batt O'Connor, *With Michael Collins in the Fight for Irish Independence*, 88.
31/1-2 J. I. C. Clarke, 'The Fighting Race,' q. Frank O'Connor, A *Book of Ireland*, 65-7.
31/4 Collins in autograph book at Frongoch, q. Seán O'Mahony, *Frongoch: University of Revolution*, 81.
32/2 Collins to Hannie, 25 August 1916.
32/4 Joe Sweeney interviewed, q. Griffith and O'Grady, *Curious Journey*, 95.
32/5 Batt O'Connor, *With Michael Collins*, 90.
33/3 Robert Brennan, *Allegiance*, 153.
33/5 Frank O'Connor, *The Big Fellow*, 37.
34/1 Collins to Hannie, 28 October 1916.
34/2 Collins to Hannie, 25 August 1916.
34/3 Collins to Seán Deasy, 12 September 1916.
34/4 O'Mahony, *Frongoch*, 19.
35/2 Collins to Hannie, 25 August 1916.
35/3 Collins to Seán Deasy, 29 September 1916.
35/4 Collins to Seán Deasy, n.d.
35/6-7 Letter from internees to T. M. Healy, 4 October, 1916, q. *Gaelic American*, 2 December, 1916.
36/1-2 *Ibid.*.
36/3 Collins to Hannie, 25 August 1916.
37/1 Collins to Deasy, 12 October 1916.
37/3 Collins to Hannie, 28 October 1916.
37/4 Richard Mulcahy, 'Conscription and the General Headquarters Staff,' *Capuchin Annual*, 1968, 35:386.
37/5 O'Mahony, *Frongoch*, 105.
37/6 *Ibid.*, 122
38/2 *Gaelic American*, 16 December 1916.
38/4 Beaslaí, *Michael Collins*, 1:114.
38/5 Collins to Seán Deasy, 22 October, 1916.
38/8-9 W. J. Brennan-Whitmore, *With the Irish in Frongoch* q. in Sir Charles Cameron, *An Autobiography*, 161.
39/1 Collins to Seán Deasy, 8 December 1916.
39/3-4 O'Mahony, *Frongoch*, 164.

Chapter 4 (pp. 40-50)
40/1 Collins to Hannie, 29 December 1916.
40/3 Rex Taylor, *Michael Collins*, 62.
40/4 Collins to Seán Deasy, n.d.

40/5 Collins to Hannie, 24 February 1917.
41/1 Collins to Seán Deasy, 19 January 17.
41/2 Collins to Hannie, 24 February 1917.
41/3 Collins to Hannie, 23 January 1917.
42/3 Collins to Thomas Ashe, 24 April 1917.
42/5 Ibid.
42/6-9 Ryan, Remembering Sion, 235.
43/3 Collins to Ashe, 24 April 1917.
43/4 Sinn Féin election poster.
44/1-4 Brennan, Allegiance, 151-2.
44/9 Collins to Nora Ashe, 22 August 1917.
45/1 Ibid.
45/3 Collins to Seán Deasy, 6 September 1917.
45/4 Collins to Hannie, 8 October 1917.
45/6 De Valera address to Ard Fheis, 25 October 1917.
46/4 Mulcahy, address, 29 October 1963.
46/5 Mulcahy, Notes on Beaslaí's Michael Collins, MS., 41.
46/6 Mulcahy, address, 29 October 1963.
47/1-2 Collins to Hannie, 10 April 1917.
47/5 Collins to Hannie, 20 April 1918.
47/6 T. Ryle, Dwyer, De Valera's Darkest Hour: In Search of National Independence, 1919-1932, 12.
48/1 Ibid.
49/4 Collins to Austin Stack, 19 August 1918.
49/5 An t-Oglach, 14 October 1918.
50/1 Batt O'Connor, With Michael Collins, 155.
50/2 Collins to de Lacy, 31 August; 14 September 1918.
50/3-4 Ernie O'Malley, On Another Man's Wound, 77.
50/6 Collins to Stack, 29 August 1918.

Chapter 5 (pp. 51-61)
51/2 Collins to Stack, November 1918.
52/3 Collins to Stack, 9 December 1918.
52/4 Collins, election address, December 1918.
53/1 Forester, Michael Collins, 97.
53/2 Collins to Stack, 15 January 1919.
53/7 Kelly, 'Escape of de Valera,' in Sworn to be Free, 35.
54/2 Collins to Stack, 9 February 1919.
54/6 Desmond Ryan, Unique Dictator, 100.
55/2 Freeman's Journal 22 March 1919.
55/4 Darrell Figgis, Recollections of the Irish War, 241.
55/5 Ibid., 243.
56/2 Earl of Longford and O'Neill, De Valera, 90.
56/4 Beaslaí, 'Twenty Got Away,' in Sworn to be Free, 50.
56/6-9 Frank O'Connor, The Big Fellow, 63.
57/2 Collins to Sister Mary Celestine Collins 13 April 1919.
57/3 Frank Pakenham, Peace by Ordeal, 39; Collins to Mary Powell, 24 April 1919.
57/5 Mulcahy, address 29 October 1963.
58/6 Frank O'Connor, The Big Fellow, 70.
59/3 Collins to Stack, 11 May 1919.
59/4 Collins to D. Hales, 16 May 1919.
60/1 Ryan, Remembering Sion, 233.
60/2 Taylor, Michael Collins, 81.
60/3 Collins to Stack, 17 and 18 May 1919.
60/4 Collins to Stack, 11 May 1919.
60/5 Collins to Stack, 17 May 1919.
61/1 Collins to Stack, 18 May 1919.
61/2 Collins to Stack, 6 June 1919.

Chapter 6 (pp. 62-73)
63/3 Batt O'Connor, *With Michael Collins*, 135.
63/5-9 Frank O'Connor, *The Big Fellow*, 49.
64/3 Ulick O'Connor, *A Terrible Beauty*, 129.
64/5-7 Collins, *The Path to Freedom*, 69-70.
65/2 *Ibid.*, 70.
65/3 Beaslaí, *Michael Collins*, 1:303.
66/5 William J. Stapelton, 'Michael Collins' Squad' *Capuchin Annual, 1969*, 370;
      Ulick O'Connor, *A Terrible Beauty*, 130.
67/1-2 Warren Fisher, report, 15 May, 1920, q. John McColgan, *British Policy and the
      Irish Administration, 1920-1922*, 8.
67/4 Collins to D. Hales, 11 September 1919.
67/6 Collins to H. Boland, 13 September 1919.
67/8 Beaslaí, *Michael Collins*, 1:342.
68/3 Forester, *Michael Collins*, 129.
68/6 Collins to D. Hales, 11 September 1919.
68/7 Collins to de Valera, 14 October 1919.
69/2 Harry Boland to Collins q. in Ó Muirthile, 'Memoirs', 78.
69/4 Dan Breen, *My Fight*, 39.
69/6 *Ibid.*, 83.
70/5 Seán Kavanagh interviewed, Griffiths and O'Grady, *Curious Journey*, 137.
71/2 Colm Connolly, 'The Shadow of Beál na mBláth,' video cassette, RTE 1989.
71/5 Beaslaí, *Michael Collins*, 1:373-4.
71/6 David Nelligan, *Spy in the Castle*, 67.
72/1 Collins to Michael Ahern, November 1919.
72/3 *Irish Times*, 1 December, 1919.
72/7 Batt O'Connor, *With Michael Collins*, 147.
73/1-2 *Ibid.*

Chapter 7 (pp. 74-83)
74/2 Report, 7 December, 1919, q. in Eunan O'Halpin, 'British Intelligence in Ireland,
      1914-21,' in Christopher Andrew and David Dilks, *The Missing Dimension*, 71.
74/4 Nelligan, *Spy in the Castle*, 107.
75/1 Brennan, *Allegiance*, 259.
75/2 Quinlisk to MacMahon, 11 November 1919, q. Beaslaí, *Michael Collins*, 1:393-
      402.
75/4 Collins to Hannie Collins, December 1919.
77/2 French to Londonderry, 3 January 1920, q. Andrew, *Secret Service*, 364.
77/5 Mulcahy, Notes on Beaslaí's *Michael Collins*, MS, 1:127.
78/3 Batt O'Connor, *With Michael Collins*, 158.
78/6 *Ibid.*, 159.
79/2 Forester, *Michael Collins*, 133.
79/4 Ulick O'Connor, *A Terrible Beauty*, 131-2.
79/5 Andrew, *Secret Service*, 366.
79/7 Collins to D. Hales, 25 February, 15 March 1920.
80/5 Ó Murithile, 'Memoirs,', 102.
80/7-8 *Ibid.*
81/4-5 Frank O'Connor, *The Big Fellow*, 92.
81/6 *Ibid.*; Thomas Jones, *Whitehall Diary*, 3:19.
81/8 see 74/2.
82/1 I.O. [C. J. C. Street], *Administration of Ireland, 1920*, 224.
82/3 *Gaelic American*, 18 September 1920.
83/1 Collins to D. Hales, 15 December 1920.

Chapter 8 (pp. 84-94)
84/3 Maurice Hankey, Diary, 30 April 1920, q. Stephen Roskill, *Man of Secrets*, 2:153.
85/1 Collins to MacSwiney, 22 March 1920.
85/2 Collins to D. Hales, 26 March 1920.
85/3 MacSwiney address q. in Con Harrington, 'Arrest and Martyrdom of Terence
      MacSwiney', *The Kerryman, Rebel's Cork Fighting Story*, 87.

86/3 Hankey, diary, 23 May 1920, q. Roskill, *Man of Secrets*, 2:153.
86/4 *Ibid.*; Thomas Jones, diary, 31 May 1920, *Whitehall Diary*, 3:17.
86/5-9 Jones, *Ibid.*, 3:17-22.
87/1-3 *Ibid.*
87-5-9 Sweeney interviewed in Griffiths and O'Grady, *Curious Journey*. 79.
87/11-12 Con Casey, 'The Shooting of Divisional Commander Smyth', in *The Kerryman, Rebel Cork's Fighting Story*, 78.
88/1-2 *Ibid.*
88/5 *Ibid.*, 80.
88/7 see 60/1.
88/8 Frank Crozier, *Ireland for Ever*, 218.
89/3 Mulcahy, 'Notes on Beaslaí's *Michael Collins*,' MS, 2:22.
89/4 *Ibid.*, 2:34.
90/2 Jones, *Whitehall Diary*, 3:28; 3:22.
90/5 Henry Wilson, diary, 1 September 1920, q. James Gleeson, *Bloody Sunday*, 110.
91/1 Collins to D. Hales, 13 August 1920.
91/3-6 *Philadelphia Public Ledger*, 26 August, 1920.
92/1 *Ibid.*.
92/3 Hankey, diary, 5 October 1920, q. Roskill, *Man of Secrets*, 2:196.
92/4 Jones, diary, 3 November 1920, *Whitehall Diary*, 3:41.
92/6 'Kevin Barry', in Waltons, *Down by the Glenside: A Selection of Irish Songs and Ballads*, 64.
93/2 Collins to Art O'Brien, 26 July 1920.
93/4-5 *The Times*, 10 November 1920.
93/6 Collins to O'Brien, 10 October 1920.

Chapter 9 (pp. 94-105)
94/3 Crozier, *Ireland for Ever*, 102.
94/4-5 Stove to King, 2 March, 1920.
94/7 Anonymous letter to MacCurtain, received 16 March 1920.
95/1 Anonymous letter to Collins, n.d., May 1920.
95/2 Beaslaí, *Michael Collins*, 1:448.
95/4 Leon O'Broin, *Michael Collins*, 57.
96/1 *Freeman's Journal*, 17 September 1920.
96/3-4 *Ibid.*
97/1 Collins to Griffith, 5 October 1920.
97/3 *New York World*, 20 October 1920.
97/4 Andrew, *Secret Service*, 367.
98/1-2 Breen, *My Fight*, 142.
98-5 *Ibid.*, 152.
98/7 Nelligan, *Spy in the Castle*, 130-1.
98/9-10 Nelligan interview in Griffiths and O'Grady, *Curious Journey*, 186.
99/2 Beaslaí, *Michael Collins*, 2:161.
99/3 Nelligan, *Spy in the Castle*, 130
99/6 Beaslaí, *Michael Collins*, 2:59; Collins to D. Hales, 18 October 1920.
100/1 Mulcahy, 'Notes on Beaslaí's *Michael Collins*,' MS, 2:31.
100/3-4 Taylor, *Michael Collins*, 104.
101/1 Ulick O'Connor, *A Terrible Beauty*, 170.
101/3-4 Seán Kavanagh interview in Griffiths and O'Grady, *Curious Journey*, 174.
102/1 Collins to Kathleen MacCormack, 7 April 1922.
102/4-5 Crozier, *Ireland for Ever*, 102.
102/6 Nelligan, *Spy in the Castle*, 123.
102/7-8 Collins, 'Notes,' q. Taylor, *Michael Collins*, 106.
103/1 Nelligan, *Spy in the Castle*, 123.
103/3 C. S. Andrews, *Dublin Made Me*, 153.
103/4 Ulick O'Connor, *A Terrible Beauty*, 172.
103/5 Andrews, *Dublin Made Me*, 153.
103/8 Daily Mail, 14 May 1921.
103/10 Hankey, diary, 25 November 1920, q. Roskill, *Man of Secrets*.
104/2 Gaughan, *Memoirs of Jeremiah Mee*, 189.
104/4 *Ibid.*

104/6 *Ibid.*
104/7 Mulcahy, 'Notes on Beaslai's *Michael Collins,*' MS, 2: 51.
104/8 Collins, note, 25 November 1920.
105/1-2 Robert Kee, *Ireland: A History*, 188.
105/5 Taylor, *Michael Collins*, 106.
105/6 O'Brien to Collins, 25 November 1920.
105/7 Collins to O'Brien, 2 December 1920.
105/8 Griffith, memo., 25 November 1920.
105/9-10 Desmond FitzGerald to D. O'Hegarty, 29 November 1920.

Chapter 10 (pp. 106-115)
106/2 Seán Ó Muirthile, 'Memoirs', MS., 125.
106/4 *Ibid.*
107/2 Sturgis diary, q. Forester, *Michael Collins*, 176.
107/3 Collins to Clune, 6 December 1920.
107/4 Collins to P. O'Keeffe, 6 December 1920.
107/6 Collins to the Editor of *Irish Independent*, 7 December 1920.
108/1-2 *Ibid.*
108/3 Art O'Brien to Collins, 9 December 1920; *The Times*, 11 December 1920.
108/5-6 Collins to Griffith, 14 December 1920.
109/2 Griffith to Collins, 14 December 1920; Jones, *Whitehall Diary*, 3: 46.
109/3 Griffith to Collins, 13 December 1920.
109/4 Collins to Art O'Brien, 15 December 1920.
110/1 Collins to Griffith, 16 December 1920.
110/3 Beaslaí, *Michael Collins*, 2: 136.
110/4 Jones, *Whitehall Dairy*, 3: 47.
110/6 *Irish Times*, 14 December 1920.
110/7 Jones, *Whitehall Dairy*, 3: 45.
110/8 *Ibid.*, 47.
111/2-5 *Ibid.*, 46.
111/8 Collins to O'Hegarty, 9 December 1920.
111/9-10 Beaslaí, *Michael Collins*, 2: 173
112/2 Forester, *Michael Collins*, 140.
112/3-5 Longford, *Peace by Ordeal*, 81.
112/7 *Ibid.*
112/9 Mulcahy, 'Notes on Beaslaí's *Michael Collins*', MS. 2: 23.
113/1 *Ibid.*, 2: 36.
113/3 Calton Younger, *Ireland's Civil War*, 95.
113/4 Tom Barry interviewed, Griffith's and O'Grady, *Curious Journey*, 169.
113/6-8 Frank O'Connor, *My Father's Son*, 117-8.
114/4 Beaslaí in *Irish Independent*, 28 August 1963.
114/6-11 Batt O'Connor, *With Michael Collins*, 170-1.
115/2 *Ibid.*, 171.

Chapter 11 (pp. 116-125)
116/2 Collins to Boland, 19 July 1919.
116/3 Collins to Stack, 20 July 1919; Collins to de Valera, 12 July 1919.
117/2 de Valera to Collins, August 1919.
117/3 Collins to de Valera, 29 August 1919.
117/6 Collins to Stack, 20 July 1919.
118/1 de Valera to Griffith, 9 July 1919.
118/4 de Valera to Grifith, 6 March 1920.
119/1 For more on de Valera and the Irish-American split, see Dwyer, *De Valera's Darkest Hour*, 30-51.
119/2 Patrick McCartan to Joe McGarrity, 12 July 1920.
119/3 Collins to H. Boland, 19 April 1920.
119/4 Flanagan to Collins q. in Collins to Griffith, 16 March 1920.
119/5 Patrick McCartan, *With de Valera in America*, 153.
120/3 *Gaelic American*, 4 and 11 September 1920.
120/4 Collins to Devoy, 30 September 1920.
120/5 Collins to Devoy, 16 October 1920.

121/4 Mulcahy, 'Notes on Beaslaí's *Michael Collins*,' MS, 2: 67.
122/1-2 de Valera to Collins, 18 January 1921.
122/4 Frank O'Connor, *The Big Fellow*, 134.
122/5 Jones, *Whitehall Diary*, 3: 47.
123/1 New York *Evening World*, 27 January 1921.
123/2 de Valera response to questionaire, q. *Gaelic American*, 26 February 1921.
123/4 de Valera to H. Boland q. in Boland to James Ó Meara, 29/2/21
123/6 Boston *American*, 29 January 1921.

Chapter 12 (pp. 126-138)
126/4 Nelligan, *Spy in the Castle*, 111.
127/2 P. S. O'Hegrty, *The Victory of Sinn Féin*, 138.
127/4 Beaslaí, *Michael Collins*, 2: 93.
127/6 *Irish Times*, 18 January 1921.
127/7-9 Beaslaí, *Michael Collins*, 2: 181.
128/1 Ormonde Winter, *Winter's Tale*, 345.
128/3 *Ibid*.
128/4-5 Collins to Sr Mary Celestine Collins, 5 March 1921.
128/6 Frank O'Connor, *The Big Fellow*, 105.
128/7 Mulcahy, 'Notes on Beaslaí's *Michael Collins*', MS, 2: 45; Beaslaí, *Michael
        Collins*, 2: 76.
129/1-3 Taylor, *Michael Collins*, 96.
130/2 Longford, *Peace by Ordeal*, 45.
130/5 Mulcahy, 'Notes on Beaslaí's *Michael Collins*', MS, 2: 73.
131/2 *Ibid.*, 45, 56.
131/5-6 Pádraig Colum, *Arthur Griffith*, 264.
132/1 de Valera to McGarrity, 21 December 1921.
132/3-4 Colum, *Arthur Griffith*, 223.
132/6 O'Broin, *Michael Collins*, 76.
132/7 Mulcahy, 'Notes on Beaslaí's *Michael Collins*', MS, 2: 84.
132/8 Collins to Q. M. 2nd Cork Brigade, 7 March 1921.
133/1 *Ibid*.
133/4 Beaslaí, *Michael Collins*, 2: 212.
134/1-2 Liam Deasy, *Towards Ireland Free: The West Cork Brigade in the War of
        Independence 1917-1921*, 256.
134/3-5 Tom Barry, *Guerrilla Days in Ireland*, 164.
134/7-14 Collins interview, *Freeman's Journal*, 22 April 1921.
135/2 Jones, *Whitehall Diary*, 3: 60.
135/4 *Ibid.*, 3: 55.
135/5 Earl of Longford and Thomas P. Ó Neill, *Eamon de Valera*, 148.
135/8 Lord Riddell, *Intimate Diary of the Peace Conference and After 1918-1923*, 288.
136/1-4 Jones, *Whitehall Diary*, 3: 68-70.
136/7 Collins to de Valera, 1 June 1921.
137/1-2 *Ibid*.
137/3 Collins to Moya Llewelyn Davies, 24 June 1921.
137/4 Collins to de Valera, 16 June 1921.
137/7 Collins, Notes, 13 July 1921, q. Taylor, *Michael Collins*, 112.
138/1 *Ibid*.

Bibliography

NOTE: Much of the research for this book is based on letters written by Michael Collins, many of which are still in private hands. I have had access to four separate private collections in the course of my research, including his own personal papers. Other letters written by him relating to the period covered in this book can be found among the papers of colleagues deposited in the National Library of Ireland, State Paper Office in Dublin Castle, the archives of University College and Trinity College, Dublin, as well as the Marquette University.

Manuscript Sources

Robert Barton: Assorted Papers, Trinity College, Dublin.
R. Erskine Childers: Papers and Diaries, Trinity College, Dublin.
Dáil Éireann: Papers in the DE2 series, State Paper Office, Dublin.
John Devoy: Papers, National Library of Ireland.
Joseph McGarrity: Papers, National Library of Ireland.
Richard Mulcahy: Papers, University College, Dublin.
Art O'Brien: Papers, National Library of Ireland.
James O'Mara: Papers, National Library of Ireland.
Ernie O'Malley: Papers, University College, Dublin.
Austin Stack: Papers, National Library of Ireland.

Published Works

Andrew, Christopher, *Secret Service: The Making of the British Intelligence Community*, London, 1985.
Andrew, C. M. and Dilks, David N., eds., *The Missing Diminsion: Government and Intelligence Communities in the Twentieth Century*, London, 1984.
Andrew, C. S., *Dublin Made Me: Autobiography*, Dublin and Cork, 1979.
Barry, Tom, *Guerrilla Days in Ireland*, Tralee, 1962.
Beaslaí Piaras, 'How it was Done – IRA Intelligence,' in *Kerryman*, ed. *Dublin's Fighting Story, 1916-1921*, Tralee, n.d.
——, *Michael Collins and the Making of the New Ireland*, 2 vols. Dublin, 1926.
——, 'Twenty Got Away,' in *Kerryman*, *Sworn to be Free*.
Breen, Dan, *My Fight for Irish Freedom*, Dublin, 1950.
Brennan, Robert, *Allegiance*, Dublin, 1950.
Brennan-Whitmore, W. J., *With the Irish in Frongoch*, Dublin, 1917.
Callwell, C. E., *Field Marshal Sir Henry Wilson: His Life and Diaries*, 2 vols. London, 1927.
Cameron, Sir Charles, *An Autobiography*, Dublin, 1920.
Carty, Xavier, *In Bloody Protest: The Tragedy of Patrick Pearse*, Dublin, 1978.
Casey, Con, 'The Shooting of Divisional Commander Smyth,' in *Rebel Cork's Fighting Story*.
Caulfield, Max, *The Easter Rebellion*, London, 1964.
Coffey, Thomas, M., *Agony at Easter: The 1916 Rising*, London, 1969.
Collins, Michael, *The Path to Freedom*, Dublin, 1922.
Colum, Pádraig, *Arthur Griffith*, Dublin 1959.
Connolly, Colm, 'The Shadow of Béal na mBláth', RTE, TV, 1989.
Crozier, Frank, *Ireland for Ever*, London, 1932.
Dáil Éireann, *Official Report: Debate on the Treaty Between Great Britain and Ireland*, Dublin, 1922.
Deasy, Liam, *Towards Ireland Free: The West Cork Brigade in the War of Independence 1917-1921*, Dublin and Cork, 1973.

Dudley, Edwards, Ruth, *Patrick Pearse: The Triumph of Failure*, London 1977.
Dwyer, T. Ryle, *De Valera's Darkest Hour: In Search of National Independence, 1919-1932*, Dublin and Cork, 1982.
Figgis, Darrell, *Recollections of the Irish War*, London, 1927.
FitzGerald, Desmond, *The Memoirs of Desmond FitzGerald*, London, 1968.
Forester, Margery, *Michael Collins: The Lost Leader*, London, 1971.
Gaughan, J. Anthony, *Austin Stack: Portrait of a Separatist*, Dublin, 1977.
——, *The Memoirs of Constable Jeremiah Mee, R.I.C.*, Dublin, 1975.
Gleeson, James, *Bloody Sunday*, London, 1962.
Griffith, Kenneth, and O'Grady, Timothy E., *Curious Journey: An Oral History of Ireland's Unfinished Revolution*, London, 1982.
Roskill, Stephen, *Hankey: Man of Secrets*, 2 vols. London, 1970-74.
Jones, Thomas, *Whitehall Diary: Volume 3: Ireland, 1918-1925*, Keith Middlemass, ed., London, 1971.
Kee, Robert, *Ireland: A History*, London, 1981.
Kelly, Bill, 'Escape of de Valera,' in *Kerryman*, ed. *Sworn to be Free*.
Kerryman, ed. *Dublin's Fighting Story, 1916-1921*, Tralee, n.d.
——, *Rebel Cork's Fighting Story: From 1916 to the Truce with Britain*, Tralee, n.d.
——, *Sworn to be Free: The Complete Book of IRA Jailbreaks, 1918-1921*, Tralee, 1971.
Longford, Earl of, and O'Neill, Thomas P., *De Valera*, London and Dublin, 1970.
Pekenham, Frank, *Peace by Ordeal*, London, 1935.
McColgan, John, *British Policy and the Irish Administration, 1920-22*, London, 1983.
MacEoin, Uinseann, ed., *Survivors*, Dublin, 1980.
McGarry, Seán, 'Michael Collins,' in *Kerryman*, ed., *Dublin's Fighting Story, 1916-1921*, Tralee, n.d.
Macready, General Sir Nevil, *Annals of an Active Life*, 2 vols., London, 1924.
Mulcahy, Richard, 'Conscription and the General Headquarters' Staff', in *Capuchin Annual, 1968*.
——, 'Chief of Staff, 1919', *The Capuchin Annual, 1969*, 340-352.
Nelligan, David, *The Spy in the Castle*, Dublin, 1968.
O'Broin, Leon, *Michael Collins*, Dublin, 1980.
O'Connor, Batt, *With Michael Collins in the Fight for Irish Independence*, London, 1929.
O'Connor, Frank, *A Book of Ireland*, London, 1959.
O'Connor, Frank, *My Father's Son*, London, 1968.
O'Connor, Frank, *The Big Fellow: Michael Collins and the Irish Revolution*, Dublin, 1965.
O'Connor, Ulick, *A Terrible Beauty*, London, 1975.
O'Halpin, Eunan, 'British Intelligence in Ireland, 1914-21,' in Christopher Andrew and David Dilks, *The Missing Dimension*.
O'Mahony, Seán, *Frongoch: University of Revolution*, Dublin, 1987.
O'Malley, Ernie, *On Another Man's Wound*, Dublin, 1936.
Pearse, Pádraic, *The Political Writings and Speeches of Patrick Pearse*, Desmond Ryan, ed., Dublin, 1966
Riddell, Lord, *Lord Riddell's Intimate Diary of the Peace Conference and After 1918-1923*, London, 1933.
Ryan, Desmond, *Remembering Sion*, London, 1934.
Ryan, Desmond, *Unique Dictator: A Study of Eamon de Valera*, London, 1936.
Stapleton, William J., 'Michael Collins' Squad,' in *The Capuchin Annual, 1969*, 368-377.
Street, C. J. C., *Administration in Ireland, 1920*, London, 1921.
——, *Ireland in 1921*, London, 1922.
Talbot, Hayden, *Michael Collins' Own Story as told to Hayden Talbot*, London, 1923.
Taylor, Rex, *Michael Collins*, London, 1958.
Townsend, Charles, *The British Campaign in Ireland, 1919-21: The Development of Political and Military Policies*, London, 1975.
——, 'The Irish Republican Army and the Development of Guerilla Warfare, 1916-1921', *English Historical Review*, 94: 318-345.
Winter, Ormonde, *Winter's Tale*, London, 1955.

Index